365 Practical and Encouraging Readings
for Sexual, Emotional, and Spiritual Integrity

EVERY WOMAN, EVERY DAY

SHANNON ETHRIDGE
WITH STEPHEN ARTERBURN

WATERBROOK

EVERY WOMAN, EVERY DAY

Quotations, adaptations, and paraphrases are taken from *Every Woman's Battle* © 2003 by Shannon Ethridge; *Every Young Woman's Battle* © 2004 by Shannon Ethridge and Stephen Arterburn; *Every Heart Restored* © 2004 by Stephen Arterburn, Brenda Stoeker, Fred Stoeker, and Mike Yorkey; and *Every Man's Battle* © 2000 by Stephen Arterburn, Fred Stoeker, and Mike Yorkey.

All Scripture quotations, unless otherwise indicated, are taken from the *Holy Bible, New International Version* ®. NIV®. Copyright © 1973, 1978, 1984 by International Bible Society. Used by permission of Zondervan Publishing House. All rights reserved. Scripture quotations marked (AMP) are taken from *The Amplified® Bible*. Copyright © 1954, 1958, 1962, 1964, 1965, 1987 by The Lockman Foundation. All rights reserved. Used by permission. (www.Lockman.org). Scripture quotations marked (MSG) are taken from *The Message*. Copyright © 1993, 1994, 1995, 1996, 2000, 2001, 2002. Used by permission of NavPress Publishing Group.

Names and facts from stories contained in this book have been changed, but the emotional and sexual struggles portrayed are true stories as related to the authors through personal interviews, letters, or e-mails.

Trade Paperback ISBN 978-0-7352-9151-5
eBook ISBN 978-0-307-50010-6

Published in the United States by WaterBrook, an imprint of the Crown Publishing Group, a division of Penguin Random House LLC, New York.

WATERBROOK® and its deer colophon are registered trademarks of Penguin Random House LLC.

2017

149062918

*I am jealous for you with a godly jealousy.
I promised you to one husband,
to Christ, so that I might present you
as a pure virgin to him. But I am afraid
that just as Eve was deceived by the
serpent's cunning, your minds may
somehow be led astray from your sincere
and pure devotion to Christ.*

2 CORINTHIANS 11:2-3

Just as sexuality isn't defined by *what we do* but by *who we are,* sexual integrity isn't defined as "not sleeping around" but as having a perfect balance between the physical, mental, emotional, and spiritual dimensions of our being.

Have there ever been seasons of your life when you focused a great deal on one of these aspects but completely neglected another one?

In order to have ultimate fulfillment and feel that physical, mental, emotional, and spiritual stability that God intended for us to have, we have to attend to each leg of our table according to God's perfect plan. If one leg is neglected, abused, or attended to in an unrighteous manner, the result is some sort of sexual compromise or emotional brokenness. When each leg is attended to or fulfilled righteously, the result is sexual integrity and emotional wholeness.

Every Woman's Battle, pages 24-25

In some way or another sexual and emotional integrity is a battle that every woman fights. However, many women are fighting this battle with their eyes closed because they don't believe they are even engaged in the battle. Many believe that just because they are not involved in a physical, sexual affair, they don't have a problem with sexual and emotional integrity. As a result, they engage in thoughts and behaviors that compromise their integrity and rob them of true sexual and emotional fulfillment.

Every Woman's Battle, page 7

*Lord, open my eyes to the battle being waged
in my heart and mind. Help me examine
my thoughts and behaviors and identify
areas in which I need to change. Thank You
for being there for me to help
me fight this battle. I want to live and act
with sexual and emotional integrity. And
I know, with Your help, that I can.*

No matter how well you try to prevent tempting thoughts from entering through the gate of your mind, some will still slip through. Life itself brings temptation. The day you stop experiencing temptation isn't the day you stop reading romance novels or watching R-rated movies or the day you put a wedding band on your finger or the day you fast and pray for twelve hours straight. The day you stop experiencing temptation is the day you die. Temptation comes part and parcel with being human, and you are no exception to that rule. Every person on the planet experiences temptation at times.

Scripture tells us that Jesus was tempted. It also tells us that He was sinless.

Jesus understands what it feels like to be tempted. He was human too. He underwent the kinds of temptations we experience, yet he did not succumb to any of them. Because we have the Holy Spirit living in us, we can have the same victory if we learn to resist temptation by redirecting our thoughts.

Every Woman's Battle, pages 79-80

As young women, we pushed the envelope while we were dating. Kissing on the first date was almost an expectation. Allowing him to go to first, second, or even third "base" was considered okay, as long as he couldn't proclaim to his friends that he'd hit a "home run" with you. But all of this sexual activity during dating didn't prepare us for true love, lifetime commitments, and faithful marriages as we thought it would. Instead, it prepared us to crave the intensity and excitement that only a new relationship brings, causing us to be discontent once we marry and the relationship ages.

When we enter marriage as "technical virgins" (having experienced most sexual pleasures with the exception of intercourse), we often face overwhelming temptations to act out sexually with another man without understanding why. The reason is simply because we never learned to nip these temptations in the bud when we were single.

If you don't learn sexual self-control as a single woman (not just physical, but emotional, mental, and spiritual self-control), you'll likely not be able to exercise it with the added stressors of two kids, a minivan, and a mortgage payment. A wedding band placed on your finger won't change you at all!

Every Woman's Battle, pages 25-26

R ecognizing and understanding what kind of things can cause every woman, regardless of her age or marital status, to stumble and fall into sexual temptation is the key. By learning to guard your mind, heart, and body against sexual compromise and understanding God's plan for your sexual and emotional fulfillment, you can maneuver your way through life with grace and without regrets.

If you have been successful in overcoming temptations thus far, praise God for His protection, and prepare for further victory. If you have given in to any of these temptations, if you wonder why you feel so disconnected from God, or if you feel anxious about your present or future relationships, our prayer is that you will find wisdom, courage, hope, and strength to face *and win* the battle for sexual and emotional integrity.

Every Young Woman's Battle, pages 14-15

He holds victory in store for the upright, he is
a shield to those whose walk is blameless, for he
guards the course of the just and protects the
way of his faithful ones. (PROVERBS 2:7-8)

If you want to win the battle for sexual integrity, you must let go of past emotional pain. Maybe a father who was absent, either emotionally or physically, wounded you. Maybe the distance in your relationship with your mother left you feeling desperately lonely. Perhaps your siblings or friends never treated you with dignity or respect. If you were abused in any way (physically, sexually, or verbally) as a child, maybe you have anger and pain that has yet to be reconciled.

Perhaps old lovers took advantage of your vulnerabilities, strung you along, or were unfaithful to you. Or maybe you've never understood why God allowed _____ to happen (you fill in the blank). Regardless of its source, you must surrender the pain from your past in order to stand strong in the battle for sexual and emotional integrity.

Every Woman's Battle, page 133

Lord, You know the pain and memories
I carry. You know every detail of these
burdens. You want to take them from me
so that I can be whole in You. Help me let
go. Help me be strong in You.

In the New Testament, Jesus reduced the Ten Commandments down to only two: " 'Love the Lord your God with all your heart and with all your soul and with all your mind.' This is the first and greatest commandment. And the second is like it: 'Love your neighbor as yourself' " (Matthew 22:37-39).

Jesus was saying that the law isn't what is important. Love is what is important. If we love God, love our neighbor, and love ourselves (in that order), then we can live far above any set of rules or regulations.

Paul echoed this form of "freedom with responsibility" when he wrote: " 'Everything is permissible'—but not everything is beneficial. 'Everything is permissible'—but not everything is constructive. Nobody should seek his own good, but the good of others' " (1 Corinthians 10:23-24).

Paul was saying that you can do most anything, but it isn't always in your best interest or in the interest of others. Focus not on what is "allowed" but on what is best for all involved.

Every Woman's Battle, pages 27-28

"Love the Lord your God with all your heart an with all your soul and with all your mind" (Matthew 22:37). Jesus doesn't say to love the Lord with whatever is left of our hearts, souls, and minds. Nor does he say God should consume our every thought every minute of the day. Most of us can't sit around all day and meditate on God. He knows you have a life. He's the one who gave it to you, and He wants you to be a good steward over your marriage relationship, your children's education, your career, your household responsibilities, your church and social commitments, and so on.

Jesus wants us to love God *more* than any of the other things that demand our time and attention.

Every Woman's Battle, pages 69-70

Lord, help me put You above all the other concerns in my life. It is so easy to get swept up in the daily routine of life and forget that You are the One who has provided it. Thank You for the blessings and the trials You have bestowed upon me. Thank You for the life You have given me. Help me make You my first priority.

Just as a man would become far more vulnerable to a sexual affair if his wife rarely responded to his physical needs for a sexual release, a woman becomes far more vulnerable to an affair when her emotional needs are neglected over and over.

When a woman falls into a sexual affair, most often her affair begins as an emotional one. It is out of her emotional needs that her heart cries out for someone to satisfy her innermost desires to be loved, needed, valued, and cherished. A woman's emotional needs are just as vitally important to her as a man's physical needs are to him.

Every Woman's Battle, page 14

Today I will take a moment to examine my emotional needs and identify them. Then I will be able to discuss them with my husband instead of blindly seeking fulfillment elsewhere.

Myth: There's nothing wrong with comparing myself, or my husband, to other people.

Truth: "When they measure themselves by themselves and compare themselves with themselves, they are not wise" (2 Corinthians 10:12).

Myth: I am mature enough to watch any movie or television show, read any book, listen to any music, or surf any Web sites without being affected in any way.

Truth: "The good [woman] brings good things out of the good stored up in [her] heart, and the evil [woman] brings evil things out of the evil stored up in [her] heart" (Luke 6:45).

Myth: It doesn't hurt anyone if I fantasize about someone other than my husband when we make love.

Truth: "The Lord does not look at the things man looks at. Man looks at the outward appearance, but the Lord looks at the heart" (1 Samuel 16:7).

Every Woman's Battle, pages 47-48

While it is common knowledge that women often compare themselves to one another and compare their husbands to other men, you may ask, "What has that got to do with sexual and emotional integrity?" To answer this question, let's first go look at the definition of a woman of integrity: Her thoughts, words, emotions, and actions all reflect an inner beauty and sincere love for God, others, and herself. When we compare ourselves to others, we put one person above the other. We either come out on top (producing vanity and pride in our lives), or we come up short (producing feelings of disappointment with what God gave us). Regardless of how we measure up when we make these comparisons, our motives are selfish and sinful rather than loving.

This opens the door to further temptations. We may experience a yearning to prove that we are more attractive than other women. Some have taken this to the extreme by landing in bed with their best friend's husband. How does this happen? It begins in a mind obsessed with comparison.

Every Woman's Battle, pages 31-32

When women compare their husbands with other men, they are toying with a threat similar to the threat a man plays with when visually lusting after other women. Whether the comparison is physical, mental, emotional, or spiritual, we not only show disrespect for our husband's uniqueness, but we also undermine our marriage and our emotional integrity. Comparisons can lead women to wonder, *Why does my husband have to be like this? Why can't he be more like so-and-so?*

Sometimes a woman will fall further into the comparison trap by entertaining more and more thoughts of so-and-so until her fantasy life becomes a world that she escapes to in order to make herself feel more valuable and loved.

When a woman's comparisons of her husband with other men heightens any disappointment or disillusionment she feels with her own husband, it can prevent her from getting excited about him sexually or emotionally. These comparisons encourage her once-glowing passion for her husband to fade to a mere tolerance of him as she forgets all about the wonderful man she fell in love with.

Every Woman's Battle, page 33

Let's face it, there will always be men more handsome, intelligent, sensitive or spiritual than our husbands, just as there will always be women slimmer, smarter, wittier, or holier than us. If "others" are the measuring stick that we use to place value on ourselves or on those we love, then we are doing exactly what Paul warns against in 2 Corinthians 10:12: "When they measure themselves by themselves and compare themselves with themselves, they are not wise." However, God gives us grace to accept others and ourselves as we really are, and He gives us the ability to truly love one another unconditionally and unreservedly. If we crave genuine intimacy, we must learn that it is only found in this kind of grace-filled relationship.

Every Woman's Battle, page 33

Lord, give me the grace to accept others as they are and to accept myself as You have made me. Comparing myself to others is so easy to do, but I know it is not beneficial to my emotional integrity. Help me keep this doorway to temptation firmly closed by being content with who I am.

The word *intimacy* itself can be best defined by breaking it into syllables, "in-to-me-see." Can we see into each other and respect, appreciate, and value what is really there, regardless of how that measures up to anyone else? That is what unconditional love and relational intimacy is all about, and it can only be discovered by two people who are seeking sexual and emotional integrity with all their minds, bodies, hearts, and souls.

Every Woman's Battle, pages 33-34

Lord, help me understand what intimacy truly is so that I will seek and desire only true intimacy and not settle for false intimacy. Also, along with desiring intimacy, help me be capable of it and not fear it.

Lord Jesus, You understand temptations. You spent forty days preparing for and facing great temptation as Satan himself presented the world to You. Temptations serve as distractions that take my attention off You. How can I learn to be closer to You in the midst of such temptation? I know I have to confess my sins, approach You humbly. I must draw upon Your light and strength, pressing into You and turning away from what tempts me. Help me focus on healthy thoughts and redirect my energy into service for others and doing work that will benefit Your kingdom.

Paul understood our very human tendency to live in denial, closing our eyes to the things in our lives that may need to change. Change is hard work, and we would rather stay as we are. But this is not how God has called us to live. He wants to help us control our minds and our desires so that we can be more like Him. He wants to help us discover His plan for relational satisfaction. But we can't do this if we insist on keeping our eyes closed to the compromise that robs us of ultimate sexual and emotional fulfillment. Open your eyes to your own struggle for sexual and emotional integrity.

Every Woman's Battle, page 15

Do not conform to the evil desires you had when you lived in ignorance. But just as he who called you is holy, so be holy in all you do; for it is written: "Be holy, because I am holy." (1 PETER 1:14-16)

Many women who struggle with sexual and/or emotional integrity are still little girls trapped in grown women's bodies, desperately seeking father figures to give them the love they craved as children. This pursuit of "love" takes the form of searching for intimacy and closeness, and unfortunately the world we live in teaches that this intimacy and closeness can only be found through sexual relationships. However, as many women have painfully discovered, relationships can be built entirely on sex and still be devoid of any intimacy or closeness at all, which leaves women feeling even more powerless to have their needs met.

These attempts to fill the father-shaped hole in their hearts through dysfunctional relationships only creates a long list of shameful liaisons and a trunk load of emotional baggage. These women are overlooking the only true source of satisfaction and self-worth: an intimate relationship with their heavenly Father. Through pursuing this relationship first and foremost, Jesus can become their first love and give them a sense of worth beyond what any man could give.

Every Woman's Battle, pages 56-57

We are not to use our bodies for the fulfillment of our own selfish desires; they are instruments through which God can do His mighty work. In order to prepare ourselves for this purpose, we must resist what the world tries to put in our minds and keep a fresh flow of godly messages coming in. That is how we will know what God wants to do through us, because then His still, small voice won't be drowned out by the blaring noise of an ungodly world.

Every Woman's Battle, page 82

Flee from sexual immorality. All other sins a man commits are outside his body, but he who sins sexually sins against his own body. Do you not know that your body is a temple of the Holy Spirit, who is in you, whom you have received from God? You are not your own; you were bought at a price. Therefore honor God with your body. (1 CORINTHIANS 6:18-20)

God created sex because of its awesome potential to draw hearts together as one and for its potency in picturing Christ's relationship with His bride, the church. You see, God never talks about sex in the context of one person, and He did not give us our sexuality for ourselves. He gave us our sexuality for our partner.

Sex is not about our individual needs. Your sexuality exists in the relationship for your husband's pleasure, and his sexuality exists in the relationship for yours. While sexual self-focus is normal everywhere else, it is not normal in the Christian marriage bed.

Every Heart Restored, pages 86-87

The husband should fulfill his marital duty to his wife, and likewise the wife to her husband. The wife's body does not belong to her alone but also to her husband. In the same way, the husband's body does not belong to him alone but also to his wife. (1 CORINTHIANS 7:3-4)

Don't fall into the trap of counseling a man about his problems if it means having isolated personal conversations, especially if one of you is married. That is what professional counselors, pastors, and his male friends are for. The only way to avoid falling into one of the many affairs that blossom in ministry and counseling offices is for men to counsel men and for women to counsel women regarding intimate issues.

Many pastors and ministry leaders refuse to counsel a woman without his wife or the woman's husband present at all times. This isn't rejection; it's wise caution.

Wisdom tells us that if we are truly going to help other people (and protect ourselves), we cannot afford to be "too good for our own good."

Every Woman's Battle, page 111

Today I will not let my nurturing nature get me into a situation that will lead to compromise.

If you invite someone to hold you accountable, you will likely be more faithful about examining the condition of your heart and mind than if you harbor things within yourself. When you fail to live up to God's standards, a wise mentor or an accountability friend can sharpen you, not with harsh judgment but with a reminder to use good judgment.

Every Young Woman's Battle, page 40

Two are better than one,
  because they have a good return
    for their work:
If one falls down,
  his friend can help him up.
But pity the man who falls
  and has no one to help him up!
    (Ecclesiastes 4:9-10)

Some women strive to gain some sense of power through inappropriate relationships with men. Rather than use what beauty God gave them to bring glory to Him, they use it as bait to lure men into feeding their egos. Rather than inspiring men to worship God, they subconsciously want men to worship them, and if they are successful in hooking a man with their charms, they secretly feel powerful.

The sense of power that will satisfy your soul is not found in *men.* It is found only in *God.* Does God give His power to men? Yes. Do you need to go through a man to receive God's power? No. The only middleman you need to tap into God's power is the Holy Spirit. And when you discover the power of the Holy Spirit to help you live an abundantly fulfilled life, you will know that seductive power pales in comparison.

Every Woman's Battle, pages 55-56

*Today I will seek the power of the Holy
Spirit instead of the adoration of men.*

One of a wife's key roles is to encourage her husband's growth and maturity as a follower of Christ, whatever that may entail. Your husband's sin is also your problem, and like it or not, you're his helper! The word *helper* in Genesis comes from a Hebrew word that means "a help as his counterpart." So what does a helper do? Helps him deal responsibly with his sexual impurity—or other sins for that matter—in any way that she can, in spite of the pain.

Every Heart Restored, pages 32-33

The LORD God said, "It is not good for the man to be alone. I will make a helper suitable for him." So the LORD God caused the man to fall into a deep sleep; and while he was sleeping, he took one of the man's ribs and closed up the place with flesh. Then the LORD God made a woman from the rib he had taken out of the man, and he brought her to the man. (GENESIS 2:18,21-22)

Women have long been using sex in order to get their own needs met. In fact, this has been going on since biblical times. Paul preached against it in his first letter to Timothy when he wrote, "I do not permit a woman to teach or to have authority over a man; she must be silent" (2:12). Some people have interpreted this verse as an injunction to keep women from any form of leadership in the church, but I believe it has nothing to do with teaching the gospel or justly exercising her authority to lead others to Christ. As I've researched the actual Greek word that Paul was using for "authority," I have come to believe he was addressing the issue of *women using sex to exert power over men.*

The word Paul uses for "authority" is the Greek word *authentein,* and not all scholars agree on its meaning. Some have translated it as "to usurp authority, domineer, or exercise authority over," but others translate it as "to involve someone in soliciting sexual liaisons." In other words, the verse could be read, "I do not permit a woman to teach sexual immorality or to involve a man in sexual sin."[1]

Every Woman's Battle, page 57

1. Kari Torjesen Malcom, *Women at the Crossroads* (Downers Grove, IL: InterVarsity, 1982), 78-79.

Once you begin stopping temptations at the gate and practice redirecting tempting thoughts, you are ready to begin the process of renewing your mind, which basically means putting new things into your brain so that you have better things to think over and meditate on. This is critical to your battle plan for becoming a woman of sexual and emotional integrity.

Every Woman's Battle, page 81

Do not conform any longer to the pattern of this world, but be transformed by the renewing of your mind. Then you will be able to test and approve what God's will is—his good, pleasing and perfect will. (ROMANS 12:2)

The problem with most of our plans to remain sexually pure or faithful within marriage is that they only include physical boundaries. Rarely do we understand the emotional progression of relationships before it's too late and we've been sucked into an affair of the heart. Because a woman can jeopardize her emotional integrity long before her body becomes vulnerable to temptation, I encourage women to focus on keeping their emotions in check. When we guard our hearts and keep them pure and faithful, we will protect our bodies as well.

Every Woman's Battle, page 25

Lord, I long to have a pure and faithful heart. Teach me to guard my heart. Teach me to recognize when I'm beginning to form unhealthy emotional attachments to someone I should not. Help me keep my emotions in check.

Perhaps some women view female sexuality as superior because it is tied to relationship and touch, while male sexuality seems baser, vulgar, and far too prone to sin.

Well, male sexuality *is* more prone to sin. But while their maleness may be *their* worst enemy in this battle for sexual purity, any superior attitudes you might have toward male sexuality may be *your* worst enemy.

The better you understand male sexuality, the more quickly and effectively your pain will dissipate. Male sexuality is complex stuff. But you absolutely must learn to view the marriage bed from the perspective of male sexual hardwiring as well as your own. To do that, you must root out any negative attitudes and accept your husband's sexuality as worthy of your tender care. If you don't, oneness won't thrive.

Every Heart Restored, pages 44-45

Consider making a covenant similar to the one Job made when he said, "I made a covenant with my eyes not to look lustfully at a girl" (Job 31:1). While most women don't lust after men's bodies (although there are certainly exceptions to this rule), we cross the line of sexual integrity in other ways. When we engage in emotional affairs, mental fantasies, and unhealthy comparisons, we are crossing the line of sexual integrity and undermining God's plan to grant us ultimate sexual and emotional fulfillment with our (current or future) husbands. We need to make a covenant with the eyes of our hearts not to look at other people (real or imagined) to fulfill our emotional needs and desires in ways that compromise our sexual integrity, whether we are married or single.

What kind of boundaries do you have in place to protect your heart, mind, and spirit in addition to your body?

Every Woman's Battle, page 26

Be wise to the ways of the world so you can guard yourself against them. Ignorance is not a spiritual gift, nor is it a virtue. You can be wise to the ways of the world and innocent at the same time. This will prepare you to make responsible decisions if and when temptations come across your path.

Every Young Woman's Battle, page 8

Lord, give me wisdom. Open my eyes to the workings of the world and the influence it is having on me. Only by understanding this can I fight against it. Help me maintain my innocence in the face of temptation. Help me fight this battle—and win.

God made every fiber and every nerve of our bodies, and He can satisfy every fiber and nerve as well. He knows how you feel and what you need better than you know yourself. He knows what will truly satisfy you—and it's not orgasm, particularly orgasm achieved through masturbation and impure thoughts. It may feel good for the moment, but it doesn't bring lasting satisfaction. That can only be found in relationship. God wants a close, intimate relationship with you. Once you allow Him to prove Himself in this area, you will understand that self-gratification was really never any gratification at all. Striving for God-gratification instead of self-gratification will ensure that your body, mind, heart, and spirit remain pure.

Every Woman's Battle, page 43

Who may ascend to the hill of the LORD?
Who may stand in his holy place?
[She] who has clean hands and a pure heart,
who does not lift up [her] soul to an idol
or swear by what is false. (PSALM 24:3-4)

Thank You, Father, for helping me see just how much I don't know about Your standard for emotional, spiritual, and sexual integrity. Thank You for new understanding about my sexuality, about things to stop doing that compromise my integrity, and about things to start doing to help me win the battle.

*If anyone considers himself religious
and yet does not keep a tight rein
on his tongue, he deceives himself
and his religion is worthless.*

JAMES 1:26

Once we connect to the ultimate source of power and discover the true power of self-control, we can take back the authority that Eve once gave to Satan. First John 4:4 reminds us that greater is He (the Holy Spirit) who is in you than he (Satan) who is in the world.

How exactly do we take this authority back? By understanding who we really are as a result of Christ's dying to set us free from the laws of sin and death. How we see ourselves affects how we live and the decisions we make. If we see ourselves as weak, tempted beyond control, or needy, then that is how we will behave. But if that is what we still believe and how we still behave, Christ's death on the cross was in vain. He died so that His Holy Spirit could fill our emptiness, heal our hurts, and satisfy our every need.

Every Woman's Battle, pages 62-63

Therefore, there is now no condemnation for those who are in Christ Jesus, because through Christ Jesus the law of the Spirit of life set me free from the law of sin and death. (ROMANS 8:1-2)

Men get their intimacy tanks filled primarily from what they do prior to and during intercourse. It is their native language of intimacy. Have you ever wondered why guys push so hard against the sexual boundaries when dating? It's not because they are godless pigs; it's because they're longing to express their hearts in their own innate language of love.

Women, on the other hand, share their intimacy in talking, sharing, hugging, and touching. However, since her sexual triggers are relational, positive relationship factors can easily draw her alongside him in her level of sexual desire. Clearly, then, these differences don't have to create problems.

But they often do. Many of us, out of pride, assume that our spouses are *choosing* to be different because they are stupid, mean, insensitive—even defective.

So it's not hard to understand why it is difficult for women to understand men and vice versa. We experience our sexuality differently than our husbands, and it's very easy to respond impatiently and ineptly by developing a prideful attitude.

Every Heart Restored, pages 62-63

It's one thing to have random sexual thoughts or inappropriate emotional longings. We are only human. God does not hold these things against us. It is another, more dangerous thing to entertain these thoughts in our minds over and over or to indulge in frequent fantasies with little regard to the nature of what is going on in our heads. Like the famous quote says,

> Sow a thought, reap an action;
> Sow an action, reap a habit;
> Sow a habit, reap a character;
> Sow a character, reap a destiny.
> —SAMUEL SMILES

You want the thoughts that you sow to reap positive actions and habits so that you can have Christlike character and fulfill the destiny God has for you.

Every Woman's Battle, pages 68-69

To be a person of integrity means that you are undivided—that all parts of your life line up with the other parts. People who believe in Jesus Christ and claim to be Christians will strive to live a life that lines up with all of Jesus's teachings. When successful in living such a life, they display integrity.

If you think being a person of sexual integrity means that you are a boring, frigid woman who never has any fun with a man, nothing can be further from the truth. A woman of sexual integrity is free to enjoy the excitement and fun of romantic relationships without all the worry that compromise brings into our lives.

Compromise is the opposite of integrity. It leads you to do things that take your mind and heart away from Christ. It usually begins in small ways but eventually blossoms into big-time sin that controls you.

So if you want to live a life of sexual integrity, you will be undivided in your devotion to sexual purity, refusing to be controlled by your sexual passions.

Every Young Woman's Battle, pages 23-24

Letting a guy know that you are interested in a more meaningful relationship with him is one thing, but inappropriate flirting, which can also be called "teasing" or "seduction," is another. Should you emotionally or physically stir up a guy if you have no intention of pursuing a relationship with him? Is it loving to tease someone with your attentions and affections if you have no desire to fulfill any hopes you may arouse in him? Showing a sincere love and respect for others allows no room for acting as if you are interested in being sexual with a guy when, in fact, you are not.

If you want to avoid setting a guy's lust aflame and to keep your own passions in check, do yourself a favor and choose your words and actions wisely.

Every Young Woman's Battle, pages 32-33

Likewise the tongue is a small part of the body, but it makes great boasts. Consider what a great forest is set on fire by a small spark. The tongue also is a fire, a world of evil among the parts of the body. It corrupts the whole person, sets the whole course of his life on fire. (JAMES 3:5-6)

Getting to know God more intimately means, in part, learning how He feels about you and understanding the provisions He has made in order to satisfy your innermost desires to feel loved, needed, and powerful (a righteous form of power, not a manipulative one). This is a great way to discover who you really are—not as the world tries to program you to be, but as your Maker designed you to be. Once you allow God to correct your beliefs about yourself, those beliefs will begin driving your decisions, your behaviors will follow directly behind, and you will have victory in this battle against sexual compromise.

Every Woman's Battle, page 64

The world doesn't fight fair. But we don't live or fight our battles that way.... The tools of our trade aren't for marketing or manipulation, but they are for demolishing that entire massively corrupt culture. We use our powerful God-tools for smashing warped philosophies, tearing down barriers erected against the truth of God, fitting every loose thought and emotion and impulse into the structure of life shaped by Christ.
(2 CORINTHIANS 10:3-5, MSG)

Are the words we choose in the best interest of the men we speak to or do they support our own private agenda? Do our thoughts seek the highest good for others, or do they serve our own dysfunctional needs and emotional cravings? Is the attention and affection we may want to express to a man going to edify him or cause him to stumble and fall into temptation?

We must look beyond the movements to the motivations behind our actions. We are each held accountable by God for what we know to do. If we want to gain the prize of sexual integrity, we may need to let go of some of our "freedoms" (in dress, thoughts, speech, and behavior) in order to serve the best interest of others out of love. God will not only provide this knowledge of how to act with integrity, He will also honor those who apply this knowledge and act with responsibility.

Every Woman's Battle, page 29

When we're standing on such moral high ground, we can even stop thinking Christianly. Some women see sexuality solely through a narrow female perspective, whether they are churchgoers or not. These women disdain any suggestion that there are differences in male sexuality that are equally valid or that wives should meet these with sacrifice and tenderness.

Believers and nonbelievers shouldn't think alike here, and if you've taken a broad brush and painted all men as perverts, that's a red flag marking a serious blind spot in your character. We cannot afford such attitudes, because it is far too damaging to our relationships.

Instead, we must try to put ourselves in their shoes and open our ears to their hearts and perspectives, and I don't think it's so hard to do. Husbands don't just ache for orgasms. They ache for their wives. But our hard attitudes can make us blind to this. We think that if we sacrifice for their need, that is enough. But it isn't. Any woman would be fighting mad if her husband sniffed away her advances by snorting, "Honey, you're like a dog in heat!"

Every Heart Restored, pages 65-67

Many women no longer govern themselves by what is absolutely true (according to Scripture) but by what is absolutely popular. Popular Morality says, "If everybody else is doing it, so can I." But let's remember what our mothers used to tell us: "If everybody else jumped off a building, would you do it?" She was right. Not everybody is doing it (it could be anything—sex outside of marriage, abortion, lesbianism, fantasy, masturbation, and so on), and even if they are, that doesn't make it the right or smart thing to do.

Every Woman's Battle, page 60

Lord, I want to be governed by what is
right, not by what is popular. And only You
can provide that knowledge. Only You can
show me what is right and what is wrong,
what will foster integrity in me and what
will lead me to compromise.

Myth: Thinking about what kind of man I'd like to have if my husband were to die is not a big deal, as long as I am not plotting how to carry that out!

Truth: "Those who live according to the sinful nature have their minds set on what that nature desires; but those who live in accordance with the Spirit have their minds set on what the Spirit desires. The mind of sinful man is death, but the mind controlled by the Spirit is life and peace; the sinful mind is hostile to God. It does not submit to God's law, nor can it do so. Those controlled by the sinful nature cannot please God. You, however, are controlled not by the sinful nature, but by the Spirit, if the Spirit of God lives in you" (Romans 8:5-9).

Myth: Masturbation does not hurt me, my relationship with my (current or future) husband, or my relationship with God.

Truth: "It is God's will that you should be sanctified: that you should avoid sexual immorality; that each of you should learn to control [her] own body in a way that is holy and honorable, not in passionate lust like the heathen, who do not know God" (1 Thessalonians 4:3-5).

Everything you choose to take in through your mind can be stored up in your heart, and it is your heart that determines the direction you will take and the choices you will make when confronted with temptation. If you fill your mind with images of sexually compromising comments and situations, you will become desensitized to similar scenarios in your own life.

A good rule of thumb is never to watch a movie or television program or read a book that you wouldn't want others to know about. If you have to keep it a secret, chances are it's going to greatly intensify your battle for sexual integrity and undermine your ultimate fulfillment.

Every Woman's Battle, page 35

Lord, please show me the areas and activities in my life that are serving only to fill my mind with images that compromise my integrity. Give me the strength to cut them out and replace them with spiritually edifying activities.

Anyone can be excited by a stranger. Everything you learn or share is new, but learning new things about a strange person is not intimacy. Intimacy is seeing what is *truly* on the inside of a person (which can only be discovered face to face over long periods of time such as what you experience in marriage).

Be careful not to mistake *intensity* for *intimacy*. Intensity fades as the newness wears off, but intimacy continues to blossom the longer you know a person.

Every Woman's Battle, page 35

Today I will not mistake the intensity of newness—of getting to know someone, of making an acquaintance—with the genuine deepness of intimacy.

The most crushing difference between the sexes is not felt in the short term but the long term. We women have healthy alternatives while we wait for our husbands to turn their hearts back to us. We have our children to raise. We can create a new web of friendships. We can bury ourselves in hobbies and church work. Our main pathway of giving and getting intimacy can be used with others in godly, healthy ways, no matter how bad it gets with our husbands. In fact these relationships and activities can become so meaningful personally that they can replace the thing you really want and make it harder to reconnect intimately with him later.

Tragically, married men have no alternative in the long term, which means we have them in a much more treacherous spot. Their language of intimacy is sex. Where do they go to build an alternative intimacy if you pull away from them? All their alternatives are sinful. When a man chooses a woman to marry, he knows he is limiting his sexual options to her alone. In the arms of this one woman, he rests the most emotionally vulnerable aspect of his being.

Every Heart Restored, pages 74-75

While avoiding unhealthy emotional connections and relationships is important, it's not enough to guarantee success in keeping our hearts guarded against compromise. The secret to ultimate emotional satisfaction is to pursue a mad, passionate love relationship with the One who made our hearts, the One who purifies our hearts, and the One who strengthens our hearts against worldly temptations. The secret is to focus our hearts on our First Love.

Every Woman's Battle, pages 98-99

Lord, help me focus my heart on You. You are my First Love, the One for me. You can fill me and satisfy my craving heart in ways beyond my wildest imagination. You can give me the strength to guard myself against the world. Only with You will I be whole and satisfied.

Lord, please give me strength to get through this fight. The battle can appear to be lost, the victory in the hands of the Enemy, but I know that You are the Divine Conqueror. You have defeated death and sin, and I can claim victory in Your mighty name. Beyond the battlefield I am taken with Your love—I am in awe of the life You have bestowed upon me. I thank You for Your daily protection and ask that You extend Your mercy on me and defend me from the perils and dangers of the night.

When we discover as young women that our curvaceous bodies or pretty faces will turn heads, it awakens us to a form of power that we may have never known as preadolescent girls. For some of us, that power is intoxicating, perhaps even addicting. Turning the head of a peer became a small thrill, while turning the head of an older, important man held huge payoffs for our egos. Whether it was the captain of the football team, the college professor, or the head of the department at work, sharing in the power of important people by aligning ourselves with them in relationship gave us a distorted sense of significance.

When men resist allowing a woman to share in their power or rob them of their personal resolve, some women have been known to become quite manipulative, using sexual prowess or emotional entanglements in order to firmly establish or hold on to their sense of power. Unfortunately, even victory in these manipulation games leaves us *power-hungry* and *powerless* over our fleshly desires.

Every Woman's Battle, page 55

What "way out" does God usually provide so that we can stand up under the temptation? Does He turn off our emotions altogether? No. Does he make the object of our desire fall off the face of the earth? No. The way out is usually provided through an accountability friendship with another woman who can sympathize with your weakness and encourage you to stand firm in the face of battle. As you give a trusted confidant permission to ask you the hard, personal questions and speak the truth in love (even if it hurts), you are required to examine the condition of your heart and mind much more than if you harbor these things within yourself.

If you think you are the only one who feels overwhelmed by sexual temptations, it will make you more vulnerable for failure because you will be less likely to ask for help to change. If this is your struggle, you can benefit from genuine intimacy in female friendships. Your friends can offer you a lifeline to hold on to when the temptation gets too deep for you to stand alone.

Every Woman's Battle, pages 46-47

Could you, like David, be so bold as to pray such a thing as this: "Test me, O LORD, and try me, examine my heart and my mind" (Psalm 26:2)?

Notice that David didn't say, "Examine my actions." He asked God to examine what was inside of him. What about you? What's on the inside of your heart and mind? Even women who have never had a serious relationship nor been involved in inappropriate sexual activity often have impure thoughts and longings. Regardless of our past, all of us share in this struggle.

Every Woman's Battle, page 68

Lord, examine me. Examine my heart and mind. I know I may not like what You find, but I must know the truth about myself so I can cooperate as You purify me.

You need to live in reality and recognize who God made you to be, and then do your best at being that person.

"But what if I don't like who I am?" you may ask. Perhaps you feel awkward, shy, or even ugly. Perhaps you desperately wish you could be someone else. With God's help you can learn to accept the things you cannot change about yourself but change the things that you can. Don't focus so much on the little, temporary things, such as the guy who doesn't know you exist or the recurring zits on your nose. Take a step back and look at the bigger picture. What do you dream about doing with your life? What are your educational, career, social service, or ministry goals? Pursue those dreams and goals with passion. You'll develop a sense of who God made you to be and you'll even grow to like that person.

Every Young Woman's Battle, pages 33-34

Turning the tide in our culture may seem like an impossible task, but we are not alone in this challenge. God will turn the tide through us. He simply asks us to submit our own lives to Him and to be witnesses to what His power and love can do. As more and more women receive this revelation and share this wisdom with others, the tide will eventually turn on its own. We need to begin by focusing on our own behaviors so that we no longer allow the world to influence us.

Every Woman's Battle, pages 61-62

Lord, how exciting it is that You can change the world through me! I want to submit my life to You and let Your Spirit guide me, instead of the world. I can't wait to see what Your power and love can do in my life and in the lives of those close to me.

Jesus Christ didn't dawdle when the time came to obey His Father's words and reclaim the world. Christ set His jaw and headed toward Jerusalem, ignoring His fear of what He knew His destiny would be—Calvary.

As His daughters, our Father is asking us to rise above our feelings and to obey His Word in the marriage bed, because therein lies *our* destiny: a God-honoring marriage based on His principles.

Every Heart Restored, page 75

He replied, "Blessed…are those who hear the word of God and obey it." (LUKE 11:28)

Being unattached has its own set of problems. Sometimes you feel lonely. You worry about what other people think of you. You contemplate your future and you fear that you'll be alone forever. But having a relationship doesn't rid you of all your problems. You are only exchanging one set of problems for a different set of problems. When you are attached, you lose the freedom of doing your own thing. You can't plan your own future because you have this other person to consider, and you still worry about what other people think of you.

You might think that one-half of a person added to one-half of another person equals one whole relationship, but this isn't true. Two people in a relationship multiply the positive and negative factors of each other. If you are wounded and incomplete, you will attract the same, and the two of you will experience a mere fraction of what God intended— and a whole lot of what He didn't.

A good relationship is more about *becoming* the right person than *finding* the right person. A healthy marriage is the union of two *already complete* people who choose to invest in each other.

Every Young Woman's Battle, pages 34-35

In most cases, your husband probably does not consciously choose cold, mechanical orgasms over relationship and oneness. Consider the possibility that with the assistance of his wiring, he's slipped into this sexual self-focus somewhat effortlessly—aided and abetted by our immoral culture and the barrage of sensual messages that clog our media.

Should you give him a pass? Not on your life. Too much is riding on it, and he is responsible to lead your family into full truth and purity. Still, don't dismiss the rest of the truth: because of nature's hardwiring, your husband will need time and the opportunity to mature spiritually so he can lead your family in this direction. Blind spots will be prevalent. But he can learn, just as so many other men have learned and made their marriages better.

So will you help him?

Every Heart Restored, page 92

Most of us become desensitized to what we see or hear. As a society, we have become so desensitized by sexual messages that we often unscrew our heads, put them under the recliner, and tolerantly allow the television to fill our minds with worldly scripts. Once our minds are corrupted, our hearts memorize these scripts, and then they seep into our lives.

Every Woman's Battle, page 34

Lord, restore my sensitivity to the corrupting
images I am bombarded with every day. I
hardly notice them anymore. I don't want
to continue being corrupted by the world's
values. I want to be filled with Your values.
Keep me aware of the influence of society,
so that I can fight against it.

Are you involved in church or a youth group? Are you working on becoming a better disciple of Christ and looking for ways to serve Him? Are you reading God's Word and praying for a deeper revelation of who God is? When you pursue God like crazy, you'll be amazed at how He molds you into someone other people are drawn to and want to get to know.

If a guy is initially drawn to your Christlike character, he likely also loves God.

Every Young Woman's Battle, page 202

> *Lord, mold me into the person You want me*
> *to be. I want to be more Christlike, not just*
> *to attract a man who loves You, but because*
> *it is what You want for me. I long to be more*
> *like You.*

While a man gets tempted sexually because of what he sees, you are more likely to be tempted sexually because your heart is crying out for someone to satisfy your innermost desires to be loved, needed, valued, and cherished. While a man also needs mental, emotional, and spiritual connection, his physical needs tend to be in the driver's seat and his other needs ride along in the back. A male can enjoy the act of sex without committing his heart or bonding spiritually with the object of his physical desire. This is the ultimate act of compartmentalization, and men are masters at it.

The reverse is true for you. A young woman's emotions are usually in the driver's seat. Never assume a guy feels what you feel.

Every Young Woman's Battle, page 19

God's Word is the only reliable standard we can use to determine if our thoughts are appropriate or inappropriate.

Every Woman's Battle, page 70

For the word of God is living and active. Sharper
than any double-edged sword, it penetrates even
to dividing soul and spirit, joints and marrow;
it judges the thoughts and attitudes of the heart.
Nothing in all creation is hidden from God's
sight. Everything is uncovered and laid bare before
the eyes of him to whom we must give account.
(HEBREWS 4:12-13)

We are to love God above anything else in this world, with as much strength and passion as each of us possibly can. We demonstrate this love for God by focusing our thoughts and energies on those things He's prepared for us to do and that are also pleasing to Him.

Does this mean God is your one and only constant thought through out the day? No. But even as you think on the various other things that demand your attention, should you be loving God with all your heart, soul, and mind? Absolutely. When we demonstrate responsible stewardship of the life He has given us, our lives offer proof of our love.

Every Woman's Battle, page 70

Whatever is true, whatever is noble, whatever is right, whatever is pure, whatever is lovely, whatever is admirable—if anything is excellent or praiseworthy—think about such things. (PHILIPPIANS 4:8)

*Holy God, You who deserve 100 percent
of my love and affection, show me the parts
of my heart that I've given away to others.
Please make my heart whole and make it
wholly Yours.*

Wisdom is better than weapons of war.

ECCLESIASTES 9:18

S exual sin flourishes in the wake of bad or broken family relationships. The splintering effects of divorce or parental death shatter our worlds. Teens, rather than feeling accepted and cherished by their parents, feel as though they've been cast aside. They spend their lives searching for love and meaning, when it should have been provided in the home by a loving mother and a loving father.

They need to be accepted and affirmed, and in the end, God is where they will find healing for their wounds and a washing away of the anger simmering in their souls.

Your heavenly Father sees you as His daughter, and He doesn't care a whit about what you have achieved or what you have done or if you are successful. All He really wants is a relationship with you, a chance to just sit down with you, and put an arm around you. Because of Jesus, you are already worthy to be called His child, a woman to be reckoned with, with nothing to prove.

Every Heart Restored, pages 110-12

The pursuit of fleshly desires will end in our ultimate demise. When we sow emotional and mental seeds of compromise, we reap a harvest of relational destruction. Emotional and mental unfaithfulness still compromise our sexual integrity.

Every Woman's Battle, pages 10-11

But each one is tempted when, by [her] own evil desire, [she] is dragged away and enticed. Then, after desire has conceived, it gives birth to sin; and sin, when it is full-grown, gives birth to death. (JAMES 1:14-15)

Either sin will keep you from the Bible, or the Bible will keep you from sin. Of course, reading or even studying the Bible won't keep you from sin. (Just look at all the pastors who are Bible scholars yet have engaged in sexual sin.) We have to *internalize* and *apply* what the Bible says.

To renew the mind means to bring fresh, living thoughts into our minds in addition to keeping old, decaying thoughts at bay. Even though it's not humanly possible to empty your mind of garbage, it is possible to crowd the garbage out by filling your mind with pure thoughts. Your mind can only concentrate on so many things at once, and the more you concentrate on wholesome thoughts, the more your unwholesome thoughts will have to take a back seat.

Every Woman's Battle, pages 83-84

Today when I catch my mind wandering
in directions it should not go, I will repeat
my favorite Bible verse and focus on God's
love instead of the garbage around me.

Sexuality is a primary communication line for transmitting and receiving intimacy. When that line goes down, the emotional life shrivels, and the effects upon marriage are disastrous.

Once the intensity of a sexual addiction takes the place of intimacy, and intimacy is then decoupled from sex, the sexual high is the end in itself. The transmitters get fried, which means the marriage bed is cooked. The souls and the spirits aren't meeting on the mattress. Only the bodies are connecting.

If you and your husband aren't really meeting in bed, there is no real relationship involved in the sexual encounter. Since a woman's sexual triggers are based on relationship, it becomes harder for her to find the desire. Without the relational connection, her husband simply doesn't arouse her anymore.

Every Heart Restored, pages 116, 118, 121

Don't make the mistake of dating a guy who needs some major repair work before you could consider him marriage material. Many women are drawn to a guy's wild, rebellious side, and then set out on a mission to mold him into the kind of man they really want him to be. We hate to break it to you, but you can't change or save anyone. Only God is in the business of doing that successfully. The research has already been done. A woman's love does not change a broken man's behavior. It only validates it. Her love says to him, "You are okay the way you are!"

Every Young Woman's Battle, page 36

Lord, forgive me for thinking that I can do Your work. Protect me from my inclination to be drawn to "fixer-uppers." Instead, mold my heart into Your image so that I will attract and be attracted to the godly man You have waiting for me.

As you dive into the things of God and go deep in your spiritual walk with Him, you will gain power over your flesh and will grow spiritually strong. The things that tempted you before will pale in comparison to the joy of walking in obedience and enjoying sweet fellowship with Christ.

Perhaps some people might think you are legalistic for not going to an R-rated movie. Your girlfriends may think you are being a stick in the mud for not going out to the singles places with them anymore. Maybe your carpool companions think you've gone too spiritual on them only listening to Christian music in the car.

But you know what will be evident in your life? You are a woman of conviction, and you live by those convictions. Others will see that your actions back up your words and that you give careful thought to the kind of woman you want to be. And if they ever come to realize that their lifestyles are not bringing them the fulfillment they long for, guess who they will likely run to for wise counsel? You guessed it: the woman who they know who can teach them how to take every thought captive and live the overcoming life!

Every Woman's Battle, pages 84-85

We do not accidentally *fall* in love or into sexual immorality. We either *dive* in that direction (passively or aggressively), or we intentionally turn the other way, refusing to cross the line between that which is fruitful and that which is forbidden. Although our emotions are very powerful, we do not have to allow them to drive our thoughts and actions into compromising situations. Instead, we can fall back on God's power to guard our hearts, driving our emotions into appropriate situations and relationships.

Every Woman's Battle, page 100

> *Lord, guard my heart. Give me the strength*
> *and will to turn my back on temptation*
> *instead of diving toward it. Help me control*
> *my emotions and keep them from sweeping*
> *me down the path of immorality.*

Intimacy Buster: having sex as a means of closeness
Intimacy Booster: having sex as a response to closeness

Intimacy Buster: requiring intimacy from your spouse
Intimacy Booster: inspiring intimacy with your spouse

Intimacy Buster: expecting your needs to be served
Intimacy Booster: serving each other's needs

Intimacy Buster: sarcastic or condescending talk
Intimacy Booster: conversing respectfully as best friends

Intimacy Buster: treating him like your child
Intimacy Booster: treating him like your husband

Every Woman's Battle, page 159

God is certainly not harsh about these things. He's merciful. He knows your frame is but dust, and He's certainly not expecting perfection from you by next Tuesday. You are, however, His little girl, His precious one, the very apple of His eye. While He would never wink at sin, He can't look at you without a little skip in His heart, either. He loved you so much that He sent a Comforter so that you would never stand alone in such times as these.

And He knows that you'll struggle some days, oscillating between compassion and anger. He knows your feelings will ebb and flow with the tide of your husband's battle, because He can't forget what it was like to walk in this same dusty flesh and to suffer utter rejection Himself. His tears are as hot as yours in this battle.

Every Heart Restored, page 127

Myth: Because I feel so sexually tempted, I must already be guilty, so why bother resisting?

Truth: "For we do not have a high priest who is unable to sympathize with our weaknesses, but we have one who has been tempted in every way, just as we are—yet was without sin. Let us then approach the throne of grace with confidence, so that we may receive mercy and find grace to help us in our time of need" (Hebrews 4:15-16).

Myth: There's no one who would really understand my struggle.

Truth: "No temptation has seized you except what is common to [woman]. And God is faithful; he will not let you be tempted beyond what you can bear. But when you are tempted, he will also provide a way out so that you can stand up under it" (1 Corinthians 10:13).

Every Woman's Battle, page 49

Just as wives have the right to be offended by our husbands' wandering eyes, men have the right to be offended by their wives' wandering minds. For women, orgasm is probably 10 percent physical and 90 percent mental. If your husband is trying to please you, he can forget about it if your mind is a million miles away, say on your grocery list. A woman must focus mentally on the sexual experience in order to derive ultimate pleasure from it.

Some women focus on the wrong things during passionate moments. They entertain thoughts of someone else. They place themselves in the middle of the plot of the romance novel they are reading. They usher in flashbacks from old lovers, previous graphic scenes they were exposed to through romance novels or pornography, or images of the latest Hollywood heartthrob. Such images rob us of the intimacy that we crave. When you fantasize about someone else when making love with your husband, you are mentally making love with another man. *He,* not your husband, is the one you feel passionate about. *He,* not your husband, is the one you feel close to emotionally.

Every Woman's Battle, pages 36-37

Trust is the basis of all relationships. There can be no one-ness and no intimacy without trust, sexual or otherwise.

Trouble is, when it comes to trust, there's a catch. No matter how desperately you want it, you can't manufacture trust on your own. Trust goes far beyond love, forgiveness, and commitment, but there is really no trick to trusting. The fact is that love, forgiveness, and commitment are choices that you can make alone in a vacuum, regardless of your husband's actions toward you. You can choose to love him simply by choosing to do so, no matter how he treats you. You can forgive him over and over even if he never asks you to. You can commit your heart faithfully to him no matter how adulterous his heart may grow in return.

But trust can't exist in a vacuum like this. Trust can only exist in relationship. Your love could be as strong as the ages, but his sin will still crush your trust and will keep crushing it until he stops.

Don't allow your husband to reframe your lack of trust in him as a referendum about your love for him. He's simply untrustworthy, and if it's a referendum about anyone's love, it would be about *his* love—for you and for God.

Every Heart Restored, pages 128-30

If some relationships in your life cause you to stumble, you may have to make some difficult decisions to end such friendships altogether, especially if the person isn't respectful of your new boundaries. Remember that the Bible tells us to *flee* from sexual immorality (1 Corinthians 6:18). If this person is holding you back from growing spiritually and becoming the godly woman you were created to be, don't hesitate to flee altogether. There is no shame in running from sin, and God will certainly honor the sacrifices you make for the sake of righteousness.

When you have a personal relationship with Jesus Christ, you have His power available to you to help you resist any temptation and make whatever changes you need to make in order to pursue a lifestyle of sexual and emotional integrity.

Every Young Woman's Battle, page 221

God gave you a role to play in every area of marriage: the role of helpmate. The principles involved in rebuilding a marriage broken by sexual sin are the same principles required to fix *any* broken marriage, regardless of the type of sin. After all, if you've been trampled by sin, you've been trampled, and it doesn't matter what kind of sin crushed your heart and marriage. A wife's response must always be the same, and she will follow the same principles of healing and restoration no matter how her husband crushed her, because the challenge is always the same: that somehow, the trust must be reestablished, real accountability must be formulated, and romantic love must be revived.

Every Heart Restored, page 135

Lord, help me fulfill my role as helpmate.
Help me to help my husband. Help us
rebuild our marriage—our trust, our love.

Jesus, help transform the challenges before me so that they will cause me to grow and give me greater insight. Make me more like You, Master, who struggled with temptation from the time You spent in the wilderness till You hung dying on the cross, assaulted with the taunt, "Come down from the cross, if you are the Son of God!"

It has been said that men use conversation as a means of communicating information, but women use conversation as a means of bonding. While communicating and bonding with our spouses, children, or female friends is great, communicating and bonding with men outside our marriage or with men we wouldn't choose to date is dangerous and often destructive. And yes, the more we communicate with a person, the more we bond, so we would do well to take a lesson from the men in this area and learn to stick to business a little better. We can learn to communicate with men in friendly but to-the-point ways that will not jeopardize our emotional integrity.

Keep your communication with other men from taking twists and turns that may ultimately lead you down the path of compromise.

Every Woman's Battle, pages 111-12

Today I will carefully monitor my conversations with men, making sure I stick to business and stay far from conversation that could lead to emotional bonding.

Rather than running to the Ultimate Healer for relief from our emotional wounds, women often make idols of relationships—worshiping a man instead of God. We begin submitting to a man's and our own unholy desires rather than submitting to God's desires for our holiness and purity, thus becoming a slave to our passions.

When we peel back the layers of emotional and sexual addiction, we can see the core problem: *doubt that God can truly satisfy our innermost needs.* So we look to a man who is not our husband, and eventually discover that he doesn't "fix" us either. If we continue this pattern of looking for love in all the wrong places, we may find that our *affairs* have progressed into full-blown *addictions.*

Every Woman's Battle, page 96

Lord, forgive me for doubting You. Forgive me for running to a man when I hurt. You are the only One who can satisfy my needs. You are the Ultimate Healer. And You are all I need.

God is the only true source of power. The only way to experience the power we crave is to connect intimately with Him. When we do, He meets our innermost needs for love, acceptance, and significance. This results in the power to exert self-control. God promises to give us self-control, along with many other attributes, when we allow ourselves to be led by the Holy Spirit.

Every Woman's Battle, page 62

But the fruit of the Spirit is love, joy, peace, patience, kindness, goodness, faithfulness, gentleness and self-control. (GALATIANS 5:22-23)

Why must we look like Jesus? The snap answer is that we're Christians, and we love Him. He is beautiful beyond description, our bright morning star. But for His purposes here on Earth, don't the reasons go deeper than that? He's not just our morning star.... He's our North Star, our reference point in this chaotic, sinful world. What does the capital *N* at the top of our moral compass stand for? That's right—it stands for *normal.*

And that's a good thing, because in this murky gloom of sexual sin, you will need your compass in the worst way. The emotional fog is thick, and the hurt and loneliness can be so disorienting that you can walk in circles for months, even years.

Jesus is your mark in the distance, your reference point. When God speaks of normal life and character, He speaks along these lines: *Jesus is My beloved Son, in whom I am well pleased. He is the most normal person ever to walk the planet Earth. You are a believer, My child. Are you walking normally like My Son, Jesus?*

You've been called to a normal life, and Jesus is the magnetic pole of all things normal. The arrow in your compass must point directly at *N.*

If you want to become a woman of sexual and emotional integrity, I urge you to ask God to help you create your own list of ways you can guard your mind against sexual temptation. Examine what you allow to come into your mind—through magazines, books, movies, television, radio, and the Internet.

Ask yourself:

- Does this glamorize ideas or values or situations that oppose my Christian values?
- Is it uplifting to my spirit, and does it make me grateful for what God has given me, or does it make me depressed and dissatisfied?
- Does this cause me to think about things that build my character, or does it tear it down?

Every Woman's Battle, page 77

Christ's example is clear. Jesus was wounded plenty, just like you—it happens to all of us. But while it's okay to *be* wounded, it's not okay to *stay* wounded.

Christ refused to stay wounded, and He didn't dwell on how He was being mistreated (as we're so prone to do). Instead, Jesus chose to be His brother's brother. He focused His woundedness at the problems around Him. By turning those wounds toward God's glory, through His pain He helped the whole world. In the end, He could pray, "I have brought you glory on earth by completing the work you gave me to do" (John 17:4).

You, too, can affect the whole world with your wounds, as long as you aim them in the right direction. You must focus your gaze on the Cross, the Word, and the regenerative power of the Holy Spirit.

Every Heart Restored, page 144

Have you ever noticed that men send one- or two-sentence e-mails, or sometimes even just one or two words? Women, on the other hand, send several lengthy paragraphs, the cutest poem that a friend forwarded recently, and a photo attachment of the family pet on their latest summer vacation. That's fine for grandma and girlfriends, but not for men who might tempt us toward forbidden or unhealthy relationships.

Many women have found cyberspace to be an extremely slippery place. Here are some guidelines for conversing in cyberspace:

- If you must contact a man for business reasons, then stick to business.
- If a man that you have a previous history with or are extremely attracted to sends you an e-mail that requires a response, be very careful not to say anything that may be interpreted as being an open door or an innuendo.
- If a man invades your space using Instant Messenger and you sense that his intentions are less than honorable, you are under no obligation to respond at all. That's what the Do Not Accept button is for.

Every Woman's Battle, pages 114-15

We must stop thinking about purity and faithfulness strictly in physical terms and understand the importance of matching our words, thoughts, actions, and convictions with God's Word. When all four of these things agree with one another and align with the Word of God, we are acting with sexual integrity. But if any one area is out of alignment with God's Word, we have compromised our sexual integrity, regardless of how far we've gone physically.

Every Woman's Battle, page 103

*Lord, don't let me live in the lie that sexual
integrity is only physical. Help me bring my
words, thoughts, and convictions in line
with Your Word. Give me the strength to
transform and renew my mind. I can be just
as sexually impure with my mind as
I can with my body.*

Have you ever counted how many references there are to fear in Scripture? Three hundred and sixty-five (one for every day of the year!) As many times as God proclaimed "fear not," it is obvious that fear is a major hindrance to the Christian life. Why is it such a hindrance? Because fear is the opposite of faith. When we focus on our fear rather than having faith in God to deliver us from evil, we are much more likely to lose the battle for sexual and emotional integrity. How can we focus on what we know God will do when we think we are doomed? Such lack of faith says to God, "Even though You've carried me this far, You are probably going to fail me now, aren't You?" Overcoming our fear and exercising our faith says to God, just as David did in Psalm 9:9-10, "The LORD is a refuge for the oppressed, a stronghold in times of trouble. Those who know your name will trust in you, for you, LORD, have never forsaken those who seek you."

Every Woman's Battle, pages 139-40

You are not just your husband's wife, called to respectfully submit to his leadership and to always be ravished in his arms. You are *also* his good Samaritan, compelled by your love to dress his wounds, and *also* his friend, taking on the "iron sharpens iron" role described in Proverbs 27:17.

That dual picture of applying the dressing and grinding the iron portrays our helper role pretty well. When we make sure to include that mental picture of applying dressings to our husbands' wounds, our primary focus remains on our own choices in the situation, rather than on our husbands', which is the second cornerstone for balanced accountability.

Every Heart Restored, page 158

Lord, help me remember that my role as a wife involves more than my happiness. It requires being a friend to my husband and helping him through his own battles.

Where does beauty really come from? This is what the Creator of beauty has to say about where it comes from and how we are to use it.

> Your beauty should not come from outward adornment, such as braided hair and the wearing of gold jewelry and fine clothes. Instead, it should be that of your inner self, the unfading beauty of a gentle and quiet spirit, which is of great worth in God's sight. For this is the way the holy women of the past who put their hope in God used to make themselves beautiful. (1 PETER 3:3-5)

Does this scripture say that we shouldn't style our hair or wear nice jewelry or clothes? Of course not. The Bible simply says that this kind of beauty fades and can't be depended upon. Physical beauty isn't going to last forever. Our primary focus shouldn't be on outward beauty. However, beauty that comes from loving and serving God with a happy heart is a beauty that endures even when your figure has fallen south and wrinkles adorn your face. True beauty comes from a heart that delights in the Lord.

Every Young Woman's Battle, pages 53-54

Intimacy Buster: hiding thoughts and fantasies
Intimacy Booster: offering mental nakedness

Intimacy Buster: making unhealthy comparisons or your
husband or yourself
Intimacy Booster: accepting each other unconditionally

Intimacy Buster: failing to use each other's love language
Intimacy Booster: learning and speaking each other's love
language

Intimacy Buster: assuming he should need a sexual release
only as often as you do
Intimacy Booster: willing to satisfy his sexual needs
according to his needs cycle

Intimacy Buster: pestering him to change his ways or
giving him the silent treatment
Intimacy Booster: praying for and with each other
consistently

Every Woman's Battle, page 159

When we limit ourselves to the "iron sharpens iron" role, we have a natural tendency to pound away at him with our iron bars, as if we are in some sort of mothering role. After all, *he's not behaving right and needs to get his little rear in gear!*

But you are not his mother, and he is not your child. He is a man, and getting his rear back into gear is not just a matter of correcting a few naughty, childish bents. Perhaps he's been wounded by years of emotional trauma, and those wounds aren't just going to skip away under your scolding. His wounds, which have become bound up with his temper and his sexuality for years, have also infiltrated his mental tapes and discolored his view of the world.

Every Heart Restored, page 158

Some of you may wish that you had learned how to fight this battle years ago, because it may have kept you from engaging in an affair. Now that you're trying to become a woman of sexual and emotional integrity, you wonder what effect your secret would have on your marriage if you were to tell your husband about it. Before you decide you will never confess an affair to your husband, ask yourself these questions:

- Is harboring these secrets ultimately as damaging to our marriage as what I did in the first place?
- Am I robbing myself and my husband of true intimacy and sexual fulfillment because of the guilt I wrestle with?
- Is my confidence that my husband loves me based on who he thinks I am—a wife who has never betrayed him?

If the answer to these questions is yes, I encourage you to look at this issue in a different light. Discovering a new level of intimacy in your marriage may be very difficult if you can't let your husband see completely into your mind and heart.

Every Woman's Battle, page 157

We must manage our expectations between short-term goals and long-term change. In the short term, for instance, you can expect *nothing* from your spouse. You might demand, "Get that temper under control," but he can't possibly reply, "Okay, sugarplum, I'll have that changed by Tuesday." Change is hard, and old habits die slowly on the battlefield.

But in the long term, you can expect *everything* from your spouse, because "[we] can do everything through [Christ] who gives [us] strength" (Philippians 4:13). In the long term, there is no wiggle room. The mate with the temper can only say, "I married my wife, for better or worse, and she traded away all her rights and freedoms to marry me. I have a responsibility to her before God to walk a godly path and to be conformed to Christ. I will not rest until my temper is under control."

Every Heart Restored, page 160

My Father and Creator, I confess my sin of wishing You had made me differently, wishing I could change everything about myself, from my hair to my feet. Please forgive me, Lord, and help me to care only that people see Your beauty in me.

You were taught, with regard to your former way of life, to put off your old self, which is being corrupted by its deceitful desires; to be made new in the attitude of your minds; and to put on the new self, created to be like God in true righteousness and holiness.

EPHESIANS 4:22-24

God longs for you to test Him and try Him so you can see Him meet all your needs. He wants to dwell in every part of your heart, not just rent a room there. He wants to fill your heart to overflowing.

Don't let guilt from past mistakes keep you from seeking a truly satisfying first-love relationship with God. He says, "Come now, let us reason together.... Though your sins are like scarlet, they shall be as white as snow; though they are red as crimson, they shall be like wool" (Isaiah 1:18). He is eager to cleanse your heart and teach you how to guard it from future pain and loneliness.

Every Woman's Battle, page 100

Lord, I want to trust You. I want You to fill the void in my heart. I want You to wash away the years of pain and fruitless seeking. And I want You to protect my heart, guard it, keep it whole and pure. Come in, Lord. There is room.

Contrary to the movie scenes you may have witnessed where one character declares to the other, "You complete me!" no human being can ever complete another. Only God can "complete" you. Yet many women try with all their power to find that special someone who will make them feel as if life is really worth living (as if living as a satisfied single person isn't possible).

No boyfriend or husband will ever make you completely happy. Period. It doesn't matter how good-looking, rich, athletic, smart, godly, or charming he may be. No man can ever make you feel like you are somebody. That comes from knowing how special you are to God and from becoming the person God created you to be. Become that person, and you will never have to look to a guy to make you happy. You won't need to, because you'll be delighted with yourself and with your life.

Every Young Woman's Battle, pages 33-34

Today, instead of depending on or searching for a man to make me happy, I will depend on God.

If you can endure the wait, there is marital joy set before you on the other side. God has such plans for your marriage!

What should you do then—just watch and pray? Not exactly. Praying for revelation is crucial, but your ministry as a helpmate stretches well past your knees. You are to enhance your husband's Christian growth, whatever that may entail. That means keeping the truth before him at all times by speaking the truth and living the truth before him.

Every Heart Restored, page 179

Let us fix our eyes on Jesus, the author and perfecter of our faith, who *for the joy* set before him *endured* the cross, scorning its shame, and sat down at the right hand of the throne of God. Consider him who endured such opposition from sinful men, so that you will not grow weary and lose heart. (HEBREWS 12:2-3, emphasis added)

While the need to love and to feel loved is a universal cry of the heart, the problem lies in where we look for this love. If we are not getting the love we need or want from a man—whether or not we have a husband—we may go searching for it. Some look in bars, and others look in business offices. Some look on college campuses, and some look in churches. Some women look to male friends, while others look to fantasy. When love eludes them, some women seek to medicate the pain of loneliness or rejection. Some take solace in food; others in sexual relationships with any willing partner. Some turn to soap operas; others to shopping.

If you have tried any of these avenues for long, you have likely come to a dead end. Your pursuit has left you longing for something greater, something deeper, something more. The good news is: God has a better way.

Every Woman's Battle, pages 86-87

It is never appropriate for a married woman to behave amorously with anyone other than her husband. If we go back to one of our definitions of a woman of integrity, you'll remember that she lives a life that lines up with her lip, and vice versa. To be loyal to our marriage partner, we must demonstrate our faithfulness not just in our actions, but also in our communication with other people. While the saying goes, "Actions speak louder than words," we can never discount the effect that words alone have on other people and on our own integrity.

Even if you do not have serious intent when you begin batting compliments or overly friendly exchanges with a man, the excitement of those ego strokes can pull you down the road toward sexual compromise, usually slowly, but sometimes at lightning speed.

Every Woman's Battle, page 105

*Lord, it is so easy for a friendly conversation
to become flirting. Help me in this area.
Keep me aware of my actions and how they
will affect both me and the men involved.
Help me use my own mouth appropriately
to protect my integrity.*

Fantasy: showering with my husband
Integrity test:

1. Is it prohibited in Scripture? No.
2. Is it beneficial? I'll bet your husband would think so.
3. Does it involve anyone else? No.

This is one thought that will enhance your sexual integrity, not compromise it.

We can use these questions as a filter for our thoughts or fantasies, as well as for anything else we expose our minds to (television, movies, books, magazines, chat rooms, music.)

Every Woman's Battle, page 72

Today I will apply this integrity test to all of my fantasies. Those that don't pass, I will quickly block from my mind.

In our quest for relational intimacy, remember there is Someone we can whisper our hearts' desires to and get our boosts from who will strengthen our integrity, not jeopardize it.

If you are thinking, *No way will talking to God ever excite me like talking to a man,* then you haven't allowed yourself to be courted by our Creator. The same God whose words possessed the power to form the entire universe longs to whisper into your hungry heart words that have the power to thrill you, heal you, and draw you into a deeper love relationship than you ever imagined possible. A guy may say that you look fine, but God's Word says, "The king is enthralled by your beauty" (Psalm 45:11). A man may tell you, "Of course I love you," but God says, "I have loved you with an everlasting love; I have drawn you with loving-kindness" (Jeremiah 31:3). Even your husband may tell you, "I'm committed to you until death," but God says, "Never will I leave you; never will I forsake you" (Hebrews 13:5).

Make time to retreat to a quiet place with the Lover of your soul. Speak whatever is on your heart, and then *listen* as God speaks straight from His heart directly to yours.

Now Joseph was well-built and handsome, and after a while his master's wife took notice of Joseph and said, "Come to bed with me!"

But he refused. "With me in charge," he told her, "my master does not concern himself with anything in the house; everything he owns he has entrusted to my care. No one is greater in this house than I am. My master has withheld nothing from me except you, because you are his wife. How then could I do such a wicked thing and sin against God?" And though she spoke to Joseph day after day, he refused to go to bed with her or even be with her. (GENESIS 39:6-10)

Can you imagine a slave being bold enough to refuse to even be in the presence of his master's wife? Obviously, Joseph knew that bad company corrupts good character. He was a man of great courage and integrity, and God eventually blessed him richly and entrusted a great deal into his care because of his integrity.

But what about you? Ask God to give you this kind of courage and integrity.

Every Woman's Battle, pages 122-23

Endurance and prayer play a part in any ministry. But remember: you are not just your husband's helper, but God's. If you expect to minister in His strength and with His heart in your helper role, getting closer to the Lord yourself is critical. According to Paul, it'll help anyone keep her head emotionally to serve the Lord well in ministry:

> But you, keep your head in all situations, endure hardship...discharge all the duties of your ministry. (2 TIMOTHY 4:5)

And make no mistake, marriage is ministry.

As you get closer to the One who created you, you'll pick up God's higher-ways view of your marriage, and that's vital. God doesn't see marriage as an end in itself but as a restorative process for both of you, and He puts us in relationships like these to allow us to work out our sin so that we can be of more use to Him.

Every Heart Restored, pages 179-80

Have you ever heard of the science experiment with a frog and hot water? The experiment goes like this: You put a frog into a pot of boiling water, and he immediately jumps out, recognizing that it isn't a safe place to be. Then, you place the same frog into a pot of room-temperature water and slowly bring the pot to a boil. What happens? The frog becomes a dinner entrée of boiled frog legs because his body gradually adjusts to the temperature of his environment. The frog is gradually desensitized (unable to feel) to the danger.

We, too, can become gradually desensitized to danger, not to the danger of boiling water but to the danger of our purity being compromised through the media.

Every Young Woman's Battle, page 123

While it is normal to think about what you would do if your husband were to die before you, mentally moving on to the next husband and entertaining thoughts of a more fulfilling future as a result of his death crosses the line of sexual and emotional integrity.

If, because you aren't happy in your marriage, you daydream about who you might marry should your husband die, be warned. You are likely to encounter the same disappointments and problems. Regardless of how great "the next guy" may be, should you ever find yourself widowed (or divorced), remember that there is a common denominator in these multiple marriages—you. If you cannot conquer pride, feelings of rejection, lust, selfishness, and laziness in this relationship and communicate your needs in such a way that inspires your husband to fill your emotional bank account, you can be sure that a different man isn't the remedy.

Put all your eggs in one basket. Invest in the relationship you've got. Focus on your marriage wholeheartedly, as if no other man existed. Assume that your spouse is the man you will grow old with. Your husband is God's gift to you. Unwrap the gift and enjoy him for as long as you have him.

Every Woman's Battle, pages 38-39

Our hearts can be just like a Velcro strip. If we leave them unprotected, we make it easy for our hearts to latch on to everyone we are attracted to. It is not enough for us to guard just our minds and bodies against sexual temptation. We also need to guard our hearts against inappropriate or forbidden relationships.

Every Woman's Battle, page 86

> *Lord, help me not to forget that sexual sin*
> *involves more than just my physical body.*
> *Help me guard my heart and refrain from*
> *becoming emotionally attached when I*
> *should not. Help me train my heart to*
> *be less like Velcro and more like Teflon.*

If your sexuality has been abused, you bear no guilt, but at the same time, it isn't okay to stay wounded. Your husband is counting on you. You are the only legitimate vessel of sexual satisfaction he has—God's promised stream of mercy and grace on his path to sexual purity (see 1 Corinthians 7:9). When you dam the stream, you have doomed him to the same struggle he so desperately tried to escape through marriage. In fact, he may be even worse off than before marriage. As a single, he could at least flee sexual temptation. Now he has a wife showering in front of him or lying next to him in a silky negligee within his grasp. She ignites his engine in a million ways, and yet she may leave him high and dry with his normal desires.

God's called you to push toward normal as his helpmate. How long are you going to avoid finding healing for your wounds? You have a responsibility to your husband sexually, and though it is rough to face that fact in light of your longstanding pain, with God's help you need to seek resolution of past hurts and move on to Normal—for your own good and joy, too.

Every Heart Restored, page 233

Women want a deep connection with a man—a connection that is so deep it grows into an inseparable intimacy that results in great satisfaction as friends as well as sexual partners. But in order for this to happen, men and women have to live lives of sexual integrity. For men, that means keeping our minds and hearts from other women, including pornographic images and sexual memories from the past. For women, that means accepting rather than rejecting their husbands. It means overcoming disappointment to keep their connection with their husbands healthy.

In order for you to grow and mature, your sexuality must be integrated into the rest of your life. That means integrating your thought life and fantasy life into your marriage. When you do, you feel complete, congruent, and whole. The danger of living in your private world of fantasy and gratification is that you end up with a segmented life, one with secret fantasies, secret sexual practices, and obsessions.

Every Woman's Battle, pages x-xi

Father, teach me to pray as Thomas à Kempis did: "We must not, therefore, despair when we are tempted but pray to God with so much the more fervor, that He may vouchsafe to help us in all tribulations, who, no doubt, according to the saying of St. Paul, will 'make such issue with the temptation, that we may be able to bear it.' Let us, therefore, humble our souls under the hand of God in all temptations and tribulations, for the humble in spirit He will save and exalt." (from The Imitation of Christ*)*

The only way to truly protect yourself from sexually transmitted diseases is to guard against sexual compromise altogether. No condom fully protects you against the physical consequences of sexually immoral behavior. Even more important, no condom protects you against the spiritual consequences of sin (broken fellowship with God). No condom will protect you from the emotional consequences of a broken heart. Therefore, don't think in terms of "safe sex," but in terms of "saving sex" until marriage or remarriage. Wise is the woman who avoids compromising behavior that can put her body at risk of disease.

Every Woman's Battle, page 126

Lord, only You can truly protect me. Help me guard myself against not only the emotional consequences of sexual sin but also the physical ones. And help me never to forget that there is more at stake than my physical health. My spiritual health and my relationship with You also suffer when I sin.

When I am justified, it is *just as if I'd* never done those things. So why do we continue beating ourselves up? Why do we allow our misery to affect our mental and physical health? You don't have to carry all that emotional baggage. Surrender your pain and your backpack full of guilt and shame; it is only making you tired and crabby. Travel light and let the joy of the Lord be your strength! Letting go of bitterness fosters healthy changes in our attitudes, promotes healthy changes in our bodies, lowers blood pressure and heart rate, boosts self-esteem, and gives feelings of hope and peace.

Every Woman's Battle, page 135

Intimacy Buster: considering sex a worldly act
Intimacy Booster: considering sex an act of worship

Intimacy Buster: giving into sex out of obligation
Intimacy Booster: initiating sex out of passionate love

Intimacy Buster: feeling personally unclean
Intimacy Booster: maintaining feminine hygiene

Intimacy Buster: darkening the room or closing eyes
    during sex
Intimacy Booster: engaging visually in sexual activity

Intimacy Buster: expressing frustration that he's "not
    doing it right"
Intimacy Booster: discussing what brings you pleasure

Every Woman's Battle, page 159

Guard your heart by:
- understanding exactly where the line is between emotional integrity and emotional compromise
- being honest with yourself and learning to recognize any hidden motives (which will tell you exactly where you stand in relationship to that line between integrity and compromise)
- pursuing a first-love relationship with Jesus Christ (once you experience a love so pure and so passionate, your heart will be strengthened in a way that you never imagined possible)

Every Woman's Battle, pages 100-101

I pray that out of his glorious riches he may strengthen you with power through his Spirit in your inner being, so that Christ may dwell in your hearts through faith. And I pray that you, being rooted and established in love, may have power, together with all the saints, to grasp how wide and long and high and deep is the love of Christ, and to know this love that surpasses knowledge—that you may be filled to the measure of all the fullness of God. (EPHESIANS 3:16-19)

For some women, underlying all of their self-pity is the belief that what Jesus did for them can't possibly be enough to rid them of their stain. They need some special miracle to set them free, and until they get that miracle, they have to beat themselves up as an act of penance.

If this rings true for you as well, then guess what? The Holy Spirit is telling you the same thing it is telling them: *Jesus opened your prison door. It's up to you to walk out!* How do you do this? By forgiving every person who has ever brought you pain, including yourself. God does not despise you for the ways you have tried to fill the void in your heart, so neither should you despise yourself.

Every Woman's Battle, page 134

Today, if I start to feel as though I am trapped in the sins of my past, I will remember that Jesus has opened the prison door—all I have to do is walk out.

Just as a table has four legs that support it, four distinct components comprise our sexuality. If one of the legs is missing or broken, it's out of balance, and the table and becomes a slide.

It's no laughing matter when one of the "legs" of our sexuality buckles, because then our lives can become a slippery slope leading to discontentment, sexual compromise, self-loathing, and emotional brokenness. When this happens, the blessing that God intended to bring richness and pleasure to our lives feels more like a curse that brings great pain and despair.

Our sexuality is comprised of four distinct aspects: the physical, mental, emotional, and spiritual dimensions of our being. These four parts combine to form the unique individual that God designed you to be. When all four aspects line up perfectly, our "tabletop" (our life) reflects balance and integrity.

Every Woman's Battle, pages 22-23

ost people make the mistake of assuming that our sexuality is limited to the physical, that we are "sexual" only when we are having sex. Nothing could be further from the truth. God designed all humans as sexual beings, whether they ever have sex or not. You were sexual the day you were conceived. You were sexual when you dressed your Barbie dolls and when you cried over your first broken heart.

By definition, our sexuality isn't *what we do.* Even people who are committed to celibacy are sexual beings. Our sexuality is *who we are,* and we were made with a body, mind, heart, and spirit, not just a body. Therefore, sexual integrity is not just about physical chastity. It is about purity in all four aspects of our being (body, mind, heart, and spirit).

Every Woman's Battle, page 23

In discussing sexual integrity, most women want a list of dos and don'ts, cans and can'ts, shoulds and shouldn'ts. They want to know: "What can I get away with? How far can I go? What's too far?"

The problem with these questions is that they are based on what is culturally and socially acceptable, which changes from place to place and from decade to decade. In the Western world, women often go out of their way to get a man's attention. In the Middle Eastern countries, women walk several paces behind the men and try to go unnoticed. Today American and European women want to know how short their skirts, shorts, or tops can be, but it wasn't that long ago that the issue of open-toed shoes was creating quite the scandal among Christians.

Therefore, a list of laws about what women of integrity can and can't wear, should and shouldn't do and say, and so on, isn't the answer. What we need is a standard of sexual integrity that will withstand the test of time as well as apply to all women of all cultures. But how can we develop a set of rules that are timeless, broad, and all-inclusive?

The answer lies not in legalism but in Christian love.

Every Woman's Battle, page 27

Don't Ask: Are my actions lawful?
Do Ask: Are my actions loving to others?

Don't Ask: Will anyone find out?
Do Ask: Is this something I'd be proud of?

Don't Ask: Would anyone condemn me?
Do Ask: Is this my highest standard?

Don't Ask: Is this socially acceptable?
Do Ask: Is this in line with my convictions?

Every Woman's Battle, page 28

Why do men ignore their role as high priest? Mostly out of laziness and natural rebelliousness. They'd rather kick back and flow with the lazy tides as long as they can do what they want.

But if they're ignoring that high priest's role out of rebelliousness, why are women ignoring their helpmate role? The answer is simple: they've been wounded by the church's silence. While their helper role is rarely supported from the pulpit, countless sermons and books pound at wives to submit, submit, submit, no matter how their husbands act and no matter how blind they have become.

And so their helper role, which might have helped strengthen husbands to become great leaders in their homes, has been stripped away from wives, while the better Christian male leadership the husbands might have provided is compromised.

Every Heart Restored, page 151

Many women are steeped in the fear of being alone, the fear of not being taken care of, the fear of not having another man on the hook in case the current one gets away. Don't let the fear of compromising tomorrow keep you from taking note and celebrating that you are standing firm today.

Don't be overwhelmed at the thought of long-term, lasting fidelity. Don't let yourself think, *Oh, there's no way I can be faithful to one man for an entire lifetime!* Consider this: "Can you be faithful for one day?" The answer is most likely: "Of course I can. One day is no big deal! It's the rest of my life that I'm worried about."

Life consists of one twenty-hour period after another. If you can be faithful for one day, you've got it made. You just do the same thing the next day and the next day.

Every Woman's Battle, pages 140-41

Today I will be faithful to my husband. Just for today. And then tomorrow I will do the same thing. And the day after tomorrow I will do the same thing.

You have probably heard gourmet chefs on the cooking channel say that when it comes to food, presentation is everything. Presentation *is* everything not just with food, but also with your body. We teach people how to treat us—with respect or disrespect by our modest or immodest dress.

The way you present yourself sends a nonverbal, but clear, message to men about how you want to be treated.

Every Woman's Battle, pages 116-18

Rather, clothe yourselves with the Lord Jesus Christ, and do not think about how to gratify the desires of the sinful nature. (ROMANS 13:14)

When you look into the mirror, what do you see? A friend or a foe? Are you thankful for God's creation or critical of His handiwork? How much time and energy do you spend critiquing and criticizing your facial features? your hair? your body? Do you compare yourself to magazine cover models or to your girlfriends, getting discouraged that you don't seem to measure up to everyone else?

Perhaps you look into the mirror often because you do like what you see—a lot. Maybe you believe that others don't measure up to you. Perhaps vanity and pride are more of an issue for you than a poor body image.

What you see in the mirror has a lot to do with what you feel in your heart.

Hopefully neither of these scenarios describes you. Hopefully you like what you see in the mirror because you are one of God's beautiful creations, but hopefully you don't let your beauty go to your head. Somewhere in between "I hate the way I look!" and "Look at me! Aren't I hot?" lies a delicate balance that you must find and maintain throughout life. Why is this so important? Because either extreme can lead you down the path of sexual compromise at lightning speed.

But perhaps you are wondering if you even *want* to cut some habits out altogether. Maybe you really *like* doing what you are doing or thinking what you are thinking.

One of the most honest prayers I've ever heard is, "Lord, forgive me for the sins that I enjoy!" Sin often feels good (at least initially), or else it wouldn't be tempting. But recognizing how your pet sins ultimately impact your life may inspire you to surrender them.

Every Woman's Battle, page 139

Lord, I must admit that I need You to for-
give me for the sins I enjoy! Open my eyes
to the affect these sins are having on me.
Help me realize once and for all why I
must cut them out of my life.

*Righteous God, I confess that I've often
wished some of my sins weren't sin. Forgive
me for embracing sin and inviting it into
my life as if it were my friend instead of my
worst enemy whose goal is to destroy me. Let
me see my sin with Your eyes and feel its
consequences with Your heart and hate it the
way You do. Help me love only You and
righteousness and what is pure and lovely.*

I will give you a new heart and put a new spirit in you; I will remove from you your heart of stone and give you a heart of flesh.

EZEKIEL 36:26

In the first chapter of Genesis we see that God created man and woman in His image and placed them in the Garden of Eden with the intention of having them rule and reign over everything. To visualize this picture, imagine God's giving Adam and Eve a beautifully wrapped gift box. Inside is a gift called *authority*. God gave this gift of authority to Adam and Eve, intending them to act wisely as stewards over all creation.

But the crafty serpent, perhaps knowing that the woman is enticed by what she hears, hissed in Eve's ear something about how she could have the power of God's wisdom if she took a bite of the forbidden fruit. Because Eve had been given authority to rule and reign over this creature, not the other way around, her response should have been to shut him up and send him packing when he tried to tempt her into disobeying God. But mesmerized by the enticement of power, Eve sank her teeth into the forbidden fruit, making the most bitter mistake of her life, a mistake which resulted in her being the one to have to pack up and leave paradise forever. Her sin was rebellion against her Creator, but the underlying tragedy was that she gave away her gift of authority to the crafty serpent.

Sometimes the truth hurts, and it's much easier if we can keep it hidden. As a matter of fact, sometimes the secrets we harbor are so painful that we don't want to face them. We assume that these secrets will go away if we don't think or talk about them with anyone. But the opposite is true. Shameful secrets fester like a splinter in a finger, and it's much better to name the secret and to let someone help us remove it from our lives so the wound will heal.

Every Young Woman's Battle, page 7

If you hold to my teaching, you are really my disciples. Then you will know the truth, and the truth will set you free. (JOHN 8:31-32)

By obsessing endlessly from the pulpit over the wife's role as "submitter" while largely ignoring her equally vital helper's role as iron sharpening iron, we've falsely inflated the *covenant* aspects of marriage (shut up and take it, no matter what) over the *relational responsibilities* of the husband to deliver oneness and intimacy to his marriage. This leaves wives to endure unspeakable emotional beatings at the hands of narrow, hardhearted husbands, with no recourse at all in the name of Christ.

Yet none of this lopsided "truth" has anything to do with Christ, and it bears no resemblance to His law of love, upon which all of God's truth hangs. As a wife, you must understand this. All of your decisions must be based upon His full Word, not upon the lopsided teaching of the church alone.

Every Heart Restored, pages 249-50

Fantasy: having a romantic candlelit dinner with Richard Gere.

Integrity test:

1. Is it prohibited in Scripture? No.
2. Is it beneficial? I can't imagine your husband would think so, nor does it make you feel more love for your husband.
3. Does it involve anyone else? Yes. This is a thought that needs to be redirected to safer ground, such as having that same dinner with your husband instead.

Every Woman's Battle, page 72

Today I will fantasize only about my husband. If any other man enters my daydreams, I will kick him out immediately.

Men look for satisfaction through sex, but physical intimacy alone doesn't bring ultimate fulfillment. Many women can attest to the fact that while a man may be fantastic in bed, that doesn't mean he fulfills her emotionally. Even great sex in marriage is not the same as genuine intimacy.

On the other hand, we women look for satisfaction through emotional connection, but this will not fulfill us unless it's celebrated through physical intimacy with our spouse. A sexless marriage resembles a friendship more than a marriage. Because sexual tension typically builds much faster for men than for women, we'll more than likely have this friendship with a very sexually frustrated husband. Even the deepest emotional connection is no substitute for genuine intimacy, either.

Genuine sexual intimacy involves all components of our sexuality—the physical, mental, emotional, and spiritual. When these four are combined, the result is an elixir that stirs the soul, heals the heart, boggles the mind, and genuinely satisfies.

Every Woman's Battle, pages 143-44

You know that men are visually stimulated at the sight of a woman's body, especially a scantily clad body. You are also aware that godly men are trying desperately to honor their wives by not allowing their eyes to stray. In light of this, if you insist on wearing clothes that reveal your sleek curves and tanned skin, are you acting lovingly or selfishly? This is a good thing to ask yourself each morning as you are getting dressed for the day. Rather than asking, "What man will I come across today and will this catch his eye?" try asking, "Would wearing this outfit be a loving expression, not causing my brothers to stumble and fall?"

Every Woman's Battle, page 120

I also want women to dress modestly, with decency and propriety, not with braided hair or gold or pearls or expensive clothes, but with good deeds, appropriate for women who profess to worship God. (1 TIMOTHY 2:9-10)

While it may be normal and healthy for young children to "discover" their sexual organs and their response to genital stimulus, there comes an age of accountability (sometime during puberty or soon thereafter) when everyone must learn sexual responsibility and self-control. When self-exploration becomes masturbation (which for females often involves sexual fantasies about others and sometimes the use of pornography), it becomes an unhealthy habit that strips a young person of sexual innocence.

Masturbation is not healthy because it can train a person to "fly solo," to operate independently of anyone else. When you masturbate, you train your body as well as your mind what to find pleasurable and how to orgasm. When you marry, if your husband isn't able to please you in the exact same way, this could make your marital sex life very frustrating and disappointing.

Most husbands find pleasure and satisfaction in bringing their wives to orgasm. If you regularly find sexual release through masturbation, you may rob your future husband of this pleasure by feeling the need to "help him."

Every Young Woman's Battle, page 145

We want our husbands to look inside of us, to pay attention to us, and to give us the emotional intimacy we crave, and we often try to force them to do so. When we attempt to require intimacy in this way, the last thing they want to do is respond to our demands (or manipulations, or however we choose to pursue it). However, there is a better way. We must inspire—not require—intimacy.

Every Woman's Battle, page 145

Today I will refrain from trying to force my husband to be emotionally intimate with me. I will try instead to inspire him to intimacy.

Imagine this: Tomorrow morning you wake up and every man on the planet has developed the ability to read your mind just by being in your presence. Does the thought make you nervous? You bet it does! Especially when we consider the thoughts that roll around in our minds on a regular basis that we would never articulate to anyone! And what if every woman developed this ability too?

Even though we can rest assured that men and women aren't likely to develop this sensitivity anytime soon, we have an even bigger concern. God has had this ability all along.

Every Woman's Battle, page 68

Lord, You can read my mind. You know every thought, every desire. Just because I never express my thoughts aloud doesn't mean You don't know. Thinking something is the same as saying it aloud, in Your eyes. Help me control my mind. Help me take my thoughts captive. It will be hard, but with Your help I can succeed.

A woman doesn't just walk up to a strange man, kiss him, and seduce him out of nowhere. But some women have done this very thing after they have known the man for some time and have entertained such thoughts in their heads over and over. Perhaps they've tested the water with a little flirting here and there to make sure he's responsive to their advances. Maybe they have even rehearsed the plan in order to make it foolproof.

Of course most women would never act out in such a blatant way. Whether the tighter reigns are a result of modesty, fear, disgust, or insecurity, many keep their affairs restricted to their minds.

But when a woman dwells on the possibility of engaging in this type of negative behavior, it can zap her strength to resist and cause her defenses to crumble.

Every Woman's Battle, pages 73-74

Believe it or not, no one has ever died from not having an orgasm. The momentary stress relief that comes from masturbating is not worth the long-term stress that the habit creates.

Masturbation hurts. It serves only to fuel our sexual fire, not quench it. When we think about doing something and play it out in our thoughts, it makes it that much easier to engage in the behavior. If a woman cannot control herself while alone, what hope does she have when some smooth-talking hunk of a man starts whispering sweet nothings into her ear?

No lust can ever be satisfied; once you begin feeding baby monsters, their appetites grow bigger and they require *more!* You are better off never feeding those monsters in the first place. If sin doesn't know you, it won't call your name! Once the sin of masturbation does know you by name, it *will* call. And call…and call…and call.

Every Woman's Battle, page 40

You can't prevent your mind from thinking random, inappropriate thoughts. But you can avoid entertaining them or dwelling on them.

In fact, you do this all the time. For example, when you arrive at an all-you-can-eat buffet, you can choose not to think about the twenty pounds you are trying to lose long enough to satisfy both your appetite and your sweet tooth, can't you? You can distract yourself with a telephone call from a friend when you have a list of house chores a mile long. Do you avoid thinking about the dirty clothes piling up in the basement when an opportunity to go shopping for new ones presents itself? Of course you do. We constantly make choices either to dwell on or disregard thoughts. We can either entertain ideas or ignore them, and sexual temptations or emotional cravings are no exception.

Every Woman's Battle, page 80

Becoming normal is what Christianity is all about. Your husband needs to become normal like Jesus and stop hurting you. At the same time, this is your chance to normalize your relationship and stop inflicting your husband with more wounds from your cold shoulder and biting tongue. The wounding on both sides has got to stop or you'll never be normal.

If you want to stand shoulder to shoulder with your husband one day in a restored marriage, a great first step is to see that you're standing shoulder to shoulder with Christ and taking on His normal, broader view of marriage as well as His normal view of your husband's sin. Without Christ at your side, you'll lack the foresight and the compassion to play your position well.

Every Heart Restored, pages 138-39

A woman's disappointment in men, circumstances, God, life, money, kids and the future can cause her heart to wander. If she's single she may turn to fantasy and self-gratification, hurting her potential to develop a healthy sexual connection with her future husband. If she's married, she may start comparing her husband with every other man, and when she does, he always comes up short. She may obsess over all that he is not and all that he could be. She may express her desires for him to be different and better, creating criticisms and complaints in almost every conversation. It becomes so serious that she begins to feel entitled to something better, someone who can meet her needs the way she deserves. Unknowingly she betrays her husband with almost every thought of him and someone else she views as superior. And with each comparison comes a greater and deeper disconnection between the two of them and the increasing likelihood that she may fall into an emotional affair or even a sexual one. But even if she does neither, her rejection of her husband destroys the potential for her to experience the fulfillment she longs for.

Every Woman's Battle, page x

Father God, I am so thankful for the good days when I revel in Your creation. The sunshine and blue skies remind me of Your desire to be present with us. I confess that I am easily distracted and forget to love You with my whole heart, even among such reminders of Your goodness and power. Please forgive my carelessness and continue to reveal Yourself in the beauty of nature and the kindness of others.

While many women flirt with men intentionally, others don't realize that their amorous comments are inappropriate. Some women are too naive to recognize the impact that their words and mannerisms have on the opposite sex. Other women are well aware, but are so hungry for affirmation that they continue to jeopardize their integrity in order to fish for compliments.

While kind words and compliments can be appropriate, we must be honest about our motives and recognize when they border on becoming manipulative or flirtatious.

Here is a list of questions to help you discern whether the words that come out of your mouth and into his ears are in his personal best interest or in the best interest of your own ego.

- What is my motive for making this comment? Is it godly?
- Am I using words to manipulate this person into a deeper relationship, into meeting my emotional needs, or into making me feel better?
- If I actually said what I am thinking about saying, then turned around to find someone standing there, would I have some explaining to do?

Every Woman's Battle, page 107

Comparison can tear out a man's heart. Guys compare the neighborhoods they live in, the cars they drive, the people they socialize with, and the families they come from. Many men struggle with this to some degree, but most will never reveal this side of themselves to their wives, even when asked. They feel trapped by their fate.

It isn't what part of town we live in that decides our fate in the end. Generally, that's something that we can't control. What we *can* control is how much hope we give to our spouse. What a husband needs is someone to look deeply into his eyes to remind him that his wife loves him and God loves him.

Every Man's Battle, page 207

Taking one day at a time and trusting our future to God is all it takes. That's why Jesus taught us to pray, "Give us this day, our daily bread." That is why God rained down bread from heaven each day when the Israelites were wandering in the desert without food—so that His people would learn daily dependence on Him. When we change our focus from the distant future to the immediate present, we gain the strength and courage to overcome the fear of what we may encounter down the road.

Every Woman's Battle, page 141

Lord, I trust my future to You. I need only
worry about today and being faithful to You.
Through You, I have the strength to over-
come my fear. My future is in Your hands,
and I know I have no need to worry.

Forgiveness is essential not just for emotional and physical healing, but also for true worship. Matthew 5:23-24 says, "Therefore, if you are offering your gift at the altar and there remember that your brother has something against you, leave your gift there in front of the altar. First go and be reconciled to your brother; then come and offer your gift." In other words, God desires our reconciliation with one another *and with ourselves* before we come to Him in worship.

When we don't forgive, we are blocked spiritually. We can't grow. In 2 Corinthians 2:10-11, Paul writes, "If you forgive anyone, I also forgive him. And what I have forgiven—if there was anything to forgive—I have forgiven in the sight of Christ for your sake, in order that Satan might not outwit us. For we are not unaware of his schemes." Here Paul warns that Satan uses unforgiveness as a tool to bring about our destruction. Forgiveness foils Satan's plots to stunt our spiritual growth.

Every Woman's Battle, page 135

To help us guard against temptation, Paul encourages Christians to put on the "full armor of God"—the belt of truth, the breastplate of righteousness, shoes of peace, the shield of faith, the helmet of salvation, and the sword of the Spirit (see Ephesians 6:13-17). We are so fortunate that the Holy Spirit gives us complete access to all of these things since truth, righteousness, peace, and faith are key ingredients to maintaining sexual and emotional integrity.

However, as we put on this full armor of God, women often fail to check for weak links that leave us open and vulnerable to temptation. Three of the most common weak links are

- compromising clothing
- compromising company
- compromising actions

Is your armor leaving you vulnerable to temptation?

Every Woman's Battle, page 116

While it's hard to grasp that sexual intimacy with you does the same thing for your husband as his "talking times" do for you, you must give the marriage bed your full attention as if you do. This is what wives need to understand. It's that simple. Life isn't a big game of chess. It's all about telling the truth about your needs and responding in love to the other. That is what marriage is made of.

Every Heart Restored, page 67

> *Lord, help me understand my husband's*
> *needs and how he expresses himself. Help me*
> *understand that sex isn't merely a physical*
> *need on his part but an emotional one, that*
> *his need is just as valid as my emotional*
> *requirements of him. Help me fulfill his*
> *needs, and help him fulfill mine.*

What is a four-letter word for a woman's favorite foreplay activity? T-A-L-K!

Think about it. What affair has ever taken place without intimate words exchanged? Women often tell me, "I've not been unfaithful to my husband. All this man and I have done is talk." But what is the nature of the words exchanged? Maybe he says things like:

- "I was hoping to see your beautiful face today."
- "Does your husband appreciate what a wonderful woman you are?"

Perhaps she responds with words like:

- "I just love being around you. You always make me feel good."
- "What would your wife say if she knew we were talking like this?"

What *would* she say? What would your husband say? "It's okay, honey. You haven't been unfaithful yet"? I don't think so. Spouses would feel very betrayed by such words. As a matter of fact, those words would probably hurt just as badly as any physical acts you could have committed, because they indicate that your heart is no longer fully invested in your marriage relationship.

Every Woman's Battle, pages 102-3

In addition to screening what you allow into your mind, you can mentally rehearse righteous responses to temptations. For instance, anytime you have inappropriate thoughts about someone or suspect that he may be coming your direction, imagine that rather than giving in and being swept away like a character in some romance novel, you actually spurn his advances. Practice what you would say in response to a man's inappropriate advances in order to communicate beyond a shadow of a doubt that you are not a woman to be toyed with or that you are not so emotionally needy that you'll cling to anyone who treats you affectionately.

Practice your righteous responses to sexual and emotional temptations so that you are able to play the part to perfection when the spotlight shines on you.

Every Woman's Battle, page 78

Today, if I catch myself rehearsing an inappropriate scene, I will instead rehearse a righteous response to the scenario.

I f we long to be women of sexual and emotional integrity, we must surrender our pride. James 4:6 reminds us that "God opposes the proud but gives grace to the humble." We can imagine what being opposed by God might look like (and shudder at the thought!). But what does God's "grace to the humble" look like? Titus 2:11-14 describes it vividly:

> For the grace of God that brings salvation has appeared to all men. It teaches us to say "No" to ungodliness and worldly passions, and to live self-controlled, upright and godly lives in this present age, while we wait for the blessed hope—the glorious appearing of our great God and Savior, Jesus Christ, who gave himself for us to redeem us from all wickedness and to purify for himself a people that are his very own, eager to do what is good.

Every Woman's Battle, page 138

C onsider implementing this practical tip for cultivating genuine intimacy in your lovemaking:

Keep a dim light on and open your eyes often while making love. You don't turn off the lights and close your eyes to feel more intimate conversing with a friend, do you? My experience has been that when it's dark or when I keep my eyes closed, I'm far more tempted to allow my mind to wander into someone else's arms. Making frequent visual contact with my husband keeps me focused on him and keeps my thoughts in the pleasurable experiences of the present, which certainly adds to my sexual fulfillment. Drink in the beauty of you and your husband engaged in the act of pleasuring each other sexually and enjoy the view.

Every Woman's Battle, page 154

If you are ever the victim of abuse or have been in the past, tell someone. Don't suffer in silence. If the person you tell doesn't believe you, tell someone else until you get some help. Don't suffer in silence.

And *do not buy into the lie that you did something to deserve abuse.* Many women never press charges against an abuser because they feel as if they may have "brought it on themselves" by something they did or said. *No one deserves to be abused, regardless of how she dresses, where she goes, or what she does.* Read that sentence again, and believe it. Even if you initiate physical involvement, you have the right to change your mind and choose not to engage in further sexual activity at any point. Of course it's wise not to put yourself in compromising situations in the first place, but even if you do, it doesn't give another person the right to abuse you.

Every Young Woman's Battle, pages 74-75

Whether it is an overly developed sense of pride in your appearance or the opposite, *either extreme can be hazardous to your sexual health.* If your vanity leads you into sexual situations with men who think you look hot, or if your poor body image causes you to latch on to any guy willing to affirm your sex appeal in spite of how you feel about yourself, you are compromising.

Many women grow up with unrealistic expectations about their bodies. It's not just Barbie dolls that create these false ideas of beauty. So do television celebrities, movie stars, magazine cover models, fashion designers, and many other aspects of today's pop culture. Far better to redefine beauty according to our Creator's definition rather than to look to the world and adopt its twisted definition.

Every Young Woman's Battle, pages 52-53

Lord, help me find a safe middle ground regarding my appearance. Fill my heart and mind with Your idea of beauty, replacing the world's standard. You made me, and You think I am beautiful. There is no compromise in that.

The heart is literally and figuratively the core of all you are and all you experience in life, so when God says to guard it above all else, He is saying, "Protect the source of your life—the physical, spiritual, and emotional source of your well-being."

Just as a lake will not be pure if its source is not pure, neither will our thoughts, words, and actions be pure if our hearts are not pure. Purity begins in our hearts. Your heart needs to be a primary concern if you hope to be a woman of sexual and emotional integrity.

Every Woman's Battle, pages 87-88

You know the next commandment pretty well, too: "Don't go to bed with another's spouse." But don't think you've preserved your virtue simply by staying out of bed. Your *heart* can be corrupted by lust even quicker than your *body.* Those leering looks [or thoughts] you think nobody notices— they are also corrupt. (MATTHEW 5:27-28, MSG)

Intimacy Buster: trying to rush orgasm by entertaining inappropriate thoughts
Intimacy Booster: savoring sexual intimacy without pressure to get it over with

Intimacy Buster: requiring orgasm as often as he ejaculates
Intimacy Booster: refraining from keeping score in the bedroom

Intimacy Buster: masturbating without your spouse
Intimacy Booster: depending totally on each other for sexual pleasure

Intimacy Buster: showing body shame and extreme inhibition
Intimacy Booster: stimulating visually with nakedness

Intimacy Buster: harboring secrets of moral failure or sexual abuse
Intimacy Booster: remaining open and honest about sexual struggles and fears

The only way to kill a bad habit is to *starve it to death.* Starving a bad habit can be painful, but not as painful as letting it rule over you. This is why Peter warned, "Dear friends, I urge you, as aliens and strangers in the world, to abstain from sinful desires, which war against your soul" (1 Peter 2:11).

Scripture also says that some things that may be permissible are still not beneficial (1 Corinthians 10:23). Your habits enslave you and bring you into bondage. That is enough reason to abstain from them all together.

But these habits are also a very proud response to our human desires. Such actions tell God, "You can't satisfy me nor is your Holy Spirit strong enough to control me. I must take care of my own physical desires." Do you hear the pride in that attitude? Do you sense the rejection of God's sovereignty and ability to help you in your time of need?

Every Woman's Battle, pages 41, 43

As much as I'm able to love someone I can't see or touch, Jesus, I love You. I know You are real. I know You are here with me and even within me, but I have to admit that sometimes I just want someone with skin on to love and love me back.

Forgive me for feeling that You aren't enough, Jesus. Would You let me feel Your touch? Would You let me know Your heart intimately? Would You help me hear Your voice? Be enough for me, Lord. Help me be satisfied in You.

*Do not offer the parts of your body to sin,
as instruments of wickedness, but rather
offer yourselves to God, as those who
have been brought from death to life;
and offer the parts of your body to him
as instruments of righteousness.*

ROMANS 6:13

We can't keep from being tempted, but we can avoid rehearsing, and we can certainly refuse to sin. No temptation becomes sin without our permission.

So how do we avoid dwelling on random thoughts to the point that we are "rehearsing" rather than "rebuking" them? There are three primary ways—the Three Rs:

- resisting
- redirecting
- renewing

Every Woman's Battle, page 75

Today I will resist those random, tempting thoughts. I will resist them and redirect them to something safe, thus renewing my mind.

Before you take aim at your husband for not meeting your emotional needs, look into your own emotional mirror and answer these questions:

- Do you know exactly what your emotional needs are yourself? (Many women don't; they just know they aren't fulfilled.)
- Have you lovingly and respectfully explained exactly what these needs are and how your husband can fill your love tank?
- Have you inspired him to try to understand your needs for emotional intimacy, or is this something you've attempted to require of him?
- How consistent have you been in meeting his physical needs (not just on special occasions, but according to his needs cycle)? Have you served his needs wholeheartedly and with a positive attitude?

Every Woman's Battle, page 150

Women desperately need encouragement and affirmation. Some perform for others to get this need met. They knock themselves out for their boss, going way above and beyond the call of duty, just so they can hear, "You did a great job." They fix themselves up all the time, dressing to arouse men and hoping to hear, "Don't you look gorgeous today!" They go out of their way to do things for people just to hear them say, "I appreciate your thoughtfulness." When you look to others for your affirmation, you have to find ways to get a fresh supply, which eventually will run you ragged. But God's affirmation will fill your emotional tank even more than any human's flattering words will. When you sense the God of the universe saying to you, "I see everything you are doing and your hard work brings me great joy; you are so beautiful to me even when you are sleeping; I see your heart and you are so very special to me," His sentiments will send you reeling further than any man ever could.

Every Woman's Battle, page 171

There will come a time when future generations will laugh at us for our "modern" thinking that men and women are the same, because the truth is—we're not. For instance, medical scientists have identified the part of the brain that drives sexual desire. The nerve bundle that trips sexual desire is usually twice the size in a man's brain as compared to a woman's.

Other structures of the brain are different as well. Male brains work quite differently from female brains. The two halves of the male brain cannot talk to each other very well, but the two halves of the female brain communicate with each other just fine. Men, then, are less able to express emotions and feelings verbally than women, generally speaking. A recent study at the Indiana University School of Medicine revealed that women use both hemispheres of the brain when listening, while men use only one.

This specialized male brain is actually advantageous to women and offers a lot to the marriage relationship. Guys can be single-minded and focused, which helps on the job front, and setbacks don't phase them as much. The problem is that this focus-oriented drive also creates obstacles to intimacy in a marriage relationship.

Every Heart Restored, pages 76-77

Catch for us the foxes,
>   the little foxes
that ruin the vineyards,
>   our vineyards that are in bloom.
>   (SONG OF SONGS 2:15)

The vineyard is a metaphor for the relationship shared between lovers. A fully blossoming vineyard symbolizes a relationship in which mental, emotional, spiritual, and physical intimacy is at its peak. But what are the foxes that ruin the vineyard a symbol of?

The foxes are the many things in your marriage which are ruining your vineyard, creating distance rather than intimacy in your marriage.

As you cultivate genuine intimacy with your husband by avoiding the intimacy busters and enjoying the intimacy boosters, you will experience the kind of mental, emotional, spiritual, and physical pleasure that God intends for your marriage relationship.

Every Woman's Battle, page 160

I f we long to be women of sexual and emotional integrity, we must understand what a mighty weapon our words are. Words are what will lead us into an affair, or words will stop an affair before it begins.

If you say, "I'm too weak to resist sexual temptation," you will be. But when God begins dealing with you and sanctifying your mouth, you'll change your tune. Start out by asking God, "Is it possible that sexual temptation could have no hold on me?" He will give you a glimmer of hope. Then begin claiming the statement, "Sexual temptation has no hold on me." After a while, you will actually begin believing it wholeheartedly. Then you can honestly declare with conviction, "Sexual temptation has no hold on me!"

If we tell ourselves that we can't resist sexual or emotional temptation, we will likely fall into temptation. But if we tell ourselves that we will not give in to sexual and emotional temptation, then we will be far more likely to back up our words with corresponding actions.

Every Woman's Battle, pages 103-4

Out of the overflow of the heart the mouth speaks. (MATTHEW 12:34)

Wives have to be careful of how their appearance can turn on other men. The Bible instructs women to dress modestly (1 Timothy 2:9), but many women tend to take such verses lightly. When shopping, some women will look for "something attractive," when they really mean "something sexy." They want the sweater that sets off their breasts, the low-cut dress that sets off their hourglass figures. While these may be nice for your husband, what about the rest of the men you know?

Every Man's Battle, page 79

Lord, help me understand how a small thing such as the clothes I wear can affect men around me. When I get dressed in the morning or go shopping, remind me of this. Help me not to compromise the integrity of my Christian brothers in such an easily avoidable way.

God *is* caring. Isn't it caring and right for God to improve your character? We *are* His, after all. What if God needs to change you by making you struggle through these problems? Is it not fair for God to ask you to serve Him this way after everything He's done for you?

Consider this verse:

> If your first concern is to look after yourself, you'll never find yourself. But if you forget about yourself and look to me, you'll find both yourself and me. (MATTHEW 10:39, MSG)

And if we don't accept His higher ways of thinking, guess what continues to happen? While you're thinking everything is wrong, everything may actually be going perfectly, from God's perspective, and you'll remain totally confused and frustrated.

Every Heart Restored, pages 142-43

If there is sexual or emotional sin in your life, you must starve it to death. You can't just "trim it down" or it will grow right back, even larger than before. Sin must be cut out completely.

But if we humbly submit to the Gardener's shears and allow Him to do the cutting, *we* can grow. We can exchange pride for humility, and begin to protect ourselves from sexual and emotional compromise.

Every Woman's Battle, page 139

Lord, I can't defeat this sin on my own.
I need You to cut it out, painful as that
may be. But I know that once it is gone,
I will be able to grow straight and strong.
I can live as You designed me to live—
emotionally and sexually pure.

A *Newsweek* cover story hailed America's newest cultural wave: a tsunami of women engaging in extramarital affairs. The primary cause? Inattentive husbands are failing to provide oneness in marriage by ignoring their wives' native language of intimacy—time, deep conversation, hugging—and stuffing their freedom to blossom as women.

As Christian women, we despise this new wave for the sake of our Lord. But if we're honest, outside of His Word we would find it pretty tough to condemn these women. We understand their needs all too well.

But what if you are the one failing to provide oneness in marriage by ignoring your husband's native language of intimacy? The parallel is exact. A wife's inattentiveness in providing regular sexual intimacy may not literally force her husband into the arms of cyberspace, but until she removes this log from her own eye, she is the last woman on earth who should be tossing stones his way. From God's viewpoint, her sin is showing.

Every Heart Restored, page 69

Jesus himself was tempted in every way. "Even sexually?" you say. Why not sexually? He was a man in every sense of the word. He had beautiful women following Him around and taking care of His needs with their own money. He was reaching out to minister to women who would have loved to have Jesus hold them in His arms. The writer didn't say, "He was tempted in every way except sexually." He was human in every way and experienced every human temptation. He set the example for us that being tempted does not mean we must give in and become slaves to our passions.

Every Woman's Battle, page 44

For we do not have a high priest who is unable to sympathize with our weaknesses, but we have one who has been tempted in every way, just as we are—yet was without sin. Let us then approach the throne of grace with confidence, so that we may receive mercy and find grace to help us in our time of need. (HEBREWS 4:15-16)

Internet relationships can be misleading and harmful to your ability to form healthy relationships with guys you interact with in person. It is hard for any real relationship to live up to the fantasy of a virtual relationship. In reality, even healthy relationships are at times disappointing, frustrating, and boring. So if a virtual relationship actually develops into a real one, that mystique will wear off and the disappointments, frustrations, and boredom of real relationships will eventually surface.

Also, in virtual relationships, your view of someone's character is one-dimensional. You see only the side that the person allows you to see. However, in real relationships, you get a more complex, three-dimensional view as you watch how a guy interacts with his parents, how he treats his little sister, how he treats his friends as well as other girls. You need to see all of these things before you can make a fair judgment about a person's true character and whether he is appealing to you or not.

In real relationships with real people, you see the whole package—the good, the bad, and the ugly.

Every Young Woman's Battle, page 63

We've all had one of those moments when some guy catches our eye for whatever reason. Perhaps you recognize there is a handsome man in the car next to yours at an intersection, or maybe you noticed one walking with long, steady strides down the street. Perhaps you have even experienced a certain amount of guilt for taking notice of these men, especially if you are married.

Should you be concerned if you notice an attractive man? Absolutely not. Have you gone against Scripture or broken any vows? No. Are you failing to guard your heart just because you notice someone is eye-appealing? No. You can rest easy in the fact that your eyes function very well, and you can simply thank God that He makes such fine art.

Every Woman's Battle, pages 88-90

Lord, thank You for the fine art the human race represents. You created each and every one of us individually. Help me not feel guilty for noticing one of your works. However, keep me from taking that awareness to the next level where it may begin to compromise me emotionally or sexually.

When asked what hinders them from making the effort to run away for a retreat with the Lord, the three most common answers women give are lack of time, lack of finances, and lack of help with the house and kids. If running away with God is something that you really want to do, you'll get creative enough to make it happen. For instance, if you feel you don't have a weekend for time alone with God, ask Him to show you ways to reprioritize to make some extended time available during the week, even if it's only a few hours. We all have the same twenty-four hours in a day, and He'll help you carve out time for such a high priority.

Every Woman's Battle, page 173

*Lord, I don't understand why waiting is
such an impossible thing for me. Time
appears to plow ahead, and the changes I
long for seem like distant dreams, whispers
of possibility, but far from present reality.
Help me understand that in the waiting
I am living my questions one day at a time.
In living the questions, I can be assured of
learning much more about Your nature than
instant answers or change will offer me.
Please give me patience and faith. Like the
rolling of the unending tide, Father, I pray
that You will continue to come upon me,
restoring my faith and granting me greater
patience for the journey.*

Do you know what you are saying about the blood that Jesus shed for you when you refuse to forgive yourself for your past? You are saying that His blood wasn't good enough for you. It didn't have enough power to cleanse you.

"Righteousness from God comes through faith in Jesus Christ to all who believe. There is no difference, for all have sinned and fall short of the glory of God, and are justified freely by his grace through the redemption that came by Christ Jesus" (Romans 3:22-24).

In other words: Righteousness does not come from perfect living, but as a gift from God. We receive this gift not by our worthiness, but simply by faith in Jesus Christ (and in the blood He shed for the redemption of our sins.) We are justified freely by God's grace—no strings attached.

Every Woman's Battle, pages 134-35

God told us to guard our hearts above all else—above our lives, our faith, our marriages, our pocketbooks, our dreams, or whatever else we hold dear. In Proverbs He tells us: "Above all else, guard your heart, for it is the wellspring of life." (4:23). Why is it so important to God that we guard our hearts?

The answer is in the word *wellspring*, which can also be interpreted as "source." The heart is the source of life. When God created us, He made our hearts central to our being—physically, spiritually, and emotionally.

Every Woman's Battle, page 87

Lord, I understand how important guarding my heart is to my well-being. The longings and desires of my heart affect every other aspect of my life. Teach me how to guard my heart, how to protect it. Teach me how to keep my heart pure. With a pure heart, I can be pure physically, spiritually, and emotionally.

While men are primarily aroused by what they see with their eyes, women are more aroused by what they hear. He may fantasize about watching a woman undress, but she fantasizes about him whispering sweet nothings in her ear. The temptation to look at pornography can be overwhelming to a male, while females would much rather read the relational dialogue in a romance novel. Men want to look and touch, whereas women much prefer to talk and relate.

Men and women struggle in different ways when it comes to sexual integrity. While a man's battle begins with what he takes in through his eyes, a woman's begins with her heart and her thoughts. A man must guard his eyes to maintain sexual integrity, but because God made women to be emotionally and mentally stimulated, we must closely guard our hearts and minds as well as our bodies if we want to experience God's plan for sexual and emotional fulfillment. A woman's battle is for sexual *and* emotional integrity.

Every Woman's Battle, pages 13-14

Once sin entered into the hearts of humans, they no longer possessed the authority to rule and reign in the world. They gave that gift to Satan when they rebelled against God. That is when Satan became the ruler of this world, simply because humanity gave him the authority.

Previously Adam and Eve had been at perfect peace in their relationship with God and with each other, but the transfer of this gift from their hands into Satan's brought all that to an end. They once felt acceptance but now felt rejection. Their sense of belonging turned to loneliness and their feelings of competence gave way to feelings of inadequacy. Their sense of identity turned to confusion and their security faded into anxiety. Whereas they once felt significance, they now felt worthlessness. Their perfect relationship with God dwindled into a spiritual void.

Every Woman's Battle, page 53

Our thoughts about our husband (whether we think about him in a negative or positive light) and our thoughts about inappropriate activities or relationships (whether we think about resisting such temptations or whether we envision ourselves engaged in these activities) can either strengthen or weaken our defenses against sexual compromise. Positive thoughts give us strength, while negative thoughts drain our strength.

When we allow our minds to envision being involved in an affair or in other inappropriate activities or relationships, we are paving the way for our defenses to become so weakened that we eventually act out our thoughts.

Sticking to our convictions, on the other hand, can give us the freedom to enjoy life without subjecting ourselves to temptations that might prove overwhelming.

Every Woman's Battle, pages 73-75

Lord, help me choose to think positively.
Instead of allowing my mind to linger on
tempting images or scenes, help me fill my head
and heart with thoughts of integrity.

If you feel you can't go away and retreat with the Lord because of household and parenting responsibilities, try explaining to your husband that you will be a much better wife and mommy if you have this time to yourself to spend with God. If you are a single mom and you cannot recruit sufficient assistance from other relatives, make a deal with a friend in a similar situation. Schedule two different weekends or other occasions where the two of you will swap houses. On the first weekend, you and your kids go to her house to keep her children and tend to her chores while she enjoys time alone with God at your house. Then when it is your turn, she'll take care of your house and kids and treat you to a getaway at her house with God.

While it's tempting to send your kids away and stay home, this never works as well because you get distracted by the mounds of laundry, rampant dust bunnies, and stacks of mail. So go somewhere. Offer to house-sit for people. If you are adventurous, go camping. Get away from the normal surroundings and routines and have a refreshing new experience with the Lord.

Every Woman's Battle, page 173

Though true beauty cannot be measured by outward appearances, looking good on the outside is relatively important because you represent God. The secret to looking and feeling your personal best is eating healthy foods and exercising your body. As you simply eat the right foods in the right amounts and exercise to enhance or maintain your metabolism and muscle strength, your body will settle into a weight that is absolutely perfect for you.

Your beauty is not "on hold" until you reach a perfect weight. You can feel beautiful at any weight, or you can be miserable until your scale reads some magical number that you may never reach or be satisfied with. The choice is yours.

Think about it. You probably know someone who looks great in her blue jeans but has such a self-centered personality or rotten attitude that "beautiful" would never be one of the words you'd use to describe her. On the other hand, you probably know a woman who may not have modeling agents beating down her door, yet she is one of the most beautiful people you know.

Every Young Woman's Battle, page 57

Do you remember the first time you felt you were in love? How he dominated your thoughts morning, noon, and night? How you could be available at a moment's notice if you knew he was coming by? Remember how you would drop anything and everything when the phone rang, desperately hoping to hear his voice on the line? The potential of this relationship's going somewhere consumed your world. No matter how hard you tried, you just couldn't get him off your mind, right? (Not that any of us tried all that hard!)

God longs for you to be that consumed with Him. Not that you can stay on an emotional mountaintop every day of your life (all love relationships go through peaks and valleys), but He desires to be your *first love.* He wants your thoughts to turn to Him throughout the good and the bad days. He wants you to watch for Him expectantly, so that you sense Him beckoning you into His presence. He aches for you to call out to Him and listen for His loving reply. Although He wants you to invest in healthy relationships with others, He wants you to be most concerned about your relationship with Him.

Every Woman's Battle, page 99

Temptations can invade our lives and eventually give birth to sin in four ways: The thoughts we choose to entertain in our minds can influence us. The words we speak or the conversations we engage in can lure us down unrighteous, dangerous paths. So can the failure to guard our hearts from getting involved in unhealthy relationships. And when we allow our bodies to be in the wrong place at the wrong time with the wrong person, we can be led toward sexual compromise.

Even if we leave only one of these doors unlocked, we are vulnerable. We must guard all four areas (our minds, our hearts, our mouths, and our bodies) if we have any hope of remaining safe and maintaining sexual integrity.

Every Woman's Battle, page 67

Today I will guard all four entries for sin,
not just one or two or three. In this way,
I will fully protect myself from sexual or
emotional compromise.

onsider implementing this practical tip for cultivating genuine intimacy in your lovemaking:

Train your brain to focus strictly on your husband during sex. Some women have had so many sexual experiences with other men that they find physical intimacy with their husband difficult to concentrate on or even boring. What a pity that we've learned to mistake intensity for intimacy. While you may think being sexual with a stranger would be more exciting, it certainly wouldn't be intimate at all, and that is what women truly crave. Intimacy occurs only as a result of knowing each other inside and out. You aren't going to fully experience that with a stranger, but only with the man you live and grow old with. If you need to train your mind to focus on your husband during sex, try meditating on the word husband or worship. Remind yourself frequently, "This is my husband. Pleasuring him sexually is an act of worship to God." Even pray during your sexual moments that God would maximize your intimacy by helping you to focus exclusively on each other.

Every Woman's Battle, page 154

James 5:16 says, "Therefore confess your sins to each other and pray for each other so that you may be healed." Obviously James felt that confession is good for the soul. While it may be dreadfully painful at first, confession is ultimately good for the marriage as well.

When you allow the person (your husband) who is most committed to loving you unconditionally to see what is truly on the inside of you, regardless of how ashamed or broken you feel over it, the rewards are endless. You can gain confidence and courage, experience healing of painful memories, and enjoy genuine intimacy with the person you love and trust the most.

Every Woman's Battle, pages 158, 160

Lord, it is hard to open up about my sins to anyone, even my husband. I am afraid of his reaction, that he will be disgusted or ashamed of me. I long for genuine intimacy, but I am afraid of what is required of me to attain it. Give me the strength and boldness to share the deepest parts of my soul with my husband, and help us deepen our relationship so we can enjoy marriage as You originally intended.

Seek a trusted friend or counselor to hold you account-able through a season of temptation. You may choose to confide in your husband because he has a vested interest in keeping you lifted up in prayer. If you don't have a husband or a friend that you can lean on during this time of trial, it would be wise to seek professional counsel. Don't assume that your problem isn't big enough to warrant taking the time to do so. Talk about it before it gets any bigger. If you know you are going to have to answer to someone else—your husband, a friend, a counselor—about your thoughts, words, and actions, you'll try harder to limit them to things you wouldn't be embarrassed to admit. Getting real and honest with yourself and with someone who can keep you from falling into the pit of compromise is the best lifeline available.

If you starve your desire to be emotionally intimate with a man, it eventually dies. The more you control your appetite for forbidden fruit, the more dignity and satisfaction you will feel about yourself and your ability to be a woman of sex-ual and emotional integrity.

Every Woman's Battle, pages 95-96

D o you need a personal revival and renewed sense of joy? Are you longing for a deeper level of intimacy and fulfillment than a husband can possibly provide? Are you ready to bask in God's special love for you and relish your role as His chosen bride? If so, carve out some special time and a special place to run away and rendezvous with your heavenly Bridegroom.

Every Woman's Battle, page 177

Your love, O LORD, reaches to the heavens,
    your faithfulness to the skies.
Your righteousness is like the mighty mountains,
    your justice like the great deep...
How priceless is your unfailing love!
Both high and low among [women] find refuge
    in the shadow of your wings.
They feast on the abundance of your house;
    you give them drink from your river of
        delights. (PSALM 36:5-9)

Here's a challenge for you: turn off your television and resist all worldly sexual messages through movies, magazines, music, the Internet, and so on for thirty days. It's okay to watch the news or something you know is squeaky clean, but if there is any question in your mind as to whether something is appropriate or not, resist it altogether for thirty days. In doing so, you will be giving your mind a break from the media's constant bombardment of sexual messages. By resisting them altogether, you will become sensitized to them once again and better able to recognize when the media is feeding you garbage.

Will you take the challenge? Spend those thirty days enjoying only media and entertainment that supports Christian values. Pray and ask God to help you see and hear things as He does. Then you'll be a true master of your media world!

As you exercise caution, use wisdom, and become a master of the media and its influences in your life, your mind will become free of the negative and degrading messages that can erode your character and endanger your ability to win the battle for sexual and emotional integrity. You'll discover that filtering unhealthy sexual messages from your life is a small price to pay for such enormous and rich rewards.

Father, thank You for making every woman similar and yet unique in so many ways. Help me be the woman You created me to be. Help me live not to satisfy my physical and emotional longings but to please You in all my thoughts and actions.

*We are the clay, you are the potter;
we are all the work of your hand.*

ISAIAH 64:8

When we first come to Christ, our spiritual life has little shape or form. We submit ourselves to Jesus Christ as our Savior and ask God to begin shaping us into what He wants us to be. As a piece of clay in God's hands, we can allow ourselves to be molded and become products of the Potter who cares for us, but we cannot express our love back to Him. We can't experience any deep sense of intimacy if we remain in this level of relationship. Why? Because a lump of clay's value is based on how it can be used. When we comply and feel God using us, we feel good about ourselves. When we mess up or don't have a clear sense of purpose, we feel guilty and distant from God. We often withdraw because we believe He is angry with us due to our poor performance. Ephesians 2:10 says, "For we are God's workmanship, created in Christ Jesus to do good works, which God prepared in advance for us to do." This scripture affirms that it is important for us to submit to God and allow Him to shape our lives into something that brings Him honor. However, He doesn't want our relationship to stagnate there. He wants it to continue growing in depth and intimacy.

Every Woman's Battle, page 164

Cherishing appears in many ways. It often manifests itself in simple, daily things rather than big romantic things. These daily acts create feelings of tenderness.

Today you may not feel cherished because of your husband's sexual sin. But in the end, women still must cherish their husbands. No sin frees husbands or wives from that responsibility.

We all struggle with sin. We all struggle with sacrificing our own visible kingdoms for God's invisible kingdom. To whatever extent your husband has won his battle against sexual sin, he deserves extra respect. But even in defeat he needs your respect. Respect is the essence of cherishing. Cherish him.

Find your husband's deepest essence and cherish him sacrificially as God did on the cross. Respect and honor him, however unrespectable he may seem. Fully give yourself to him.

Every Man's Battle, pages 207-9

Any husband ought to know that he is to treat his wife with tenderness as a fellow heir to the kingdom of grace (see 1 Peter 3:7), and doing so makes it far easier for her to desire him. He also ought to know that since God never spoke of sexuality outside of the context of two, He did not give us our sexuality for ourselves. Our sexuality was given to us primarily for our partner's pleasure, not for our own. That can only mean one thing: a husband is wrong to use 1 Corinthians 7:3-4 to fight for *his* rights, and instead he should be using it to fight for *your* rights.

Every Heart Restored, pages 228-29

Women often make the mistake of believing that because they are so attracted to someone, they will inevitably fall into a relationship with that person, regardless of how inappropriate that relationship may be. Women can draw a line between attraction and acting on that attraction. It is normal to feel attracted to multiple people. It is *not* normal to attach yourself to multiple people. Remember that love is not a feeling, but a commitment. You've not broken your commitment to your husband if you feel tempted to seek satisfaction outside your marriage, but only when you've allowed yourself to stray there and stay there mentally, emotionally, or physically.

Every Woman's Battle, page 45

Lord, help me understand that I do not need to pursue or dwell upon the attraction I may feel for a man. Instead I should focus on my commitment to my husband—my commitment to love him. If I am seeking satisfaction, I need to come to You. You are the only One who can fulfill my needs.

As you struggle with your emotions to fully understand your husband's sexual "problem" and its effects on your marriage, realize that something just as harmful to marriage as sexual sin is the sin of comparison. When men look at sensual things, it can make them less satisfied with their wives. Likewise when women fantasize about the perfect husband, it can make them less satisfied with the mate God has given them.

Women are susceptible to this in different ways. Some fall prey to comparing their now-stodgy husband to the "hunk" they once knew in college. For others, the dissatisfaction comes from dreaming of a fling to far-off island, or reading a romance novel and responding with "if only" feelings that lead only to dissatisfaction.

Every Man's Battle, page 80

Fantasy: waking up in my husband's arms on a tropical vacation.

Integrity test:

1. Is it prohibited in Scripture? Certainly not.
2. Is it beneficial? You bet.
3. Does it involve anyone else? No.

This dream is okay to hold on to.

Every Woman's Battle, page 72

Lord, help me replace my inappropriate fantasies with ones such as this. Help me be so delighted and excited about my husband that I can't help thinking about him.

We walk through the produce section and notice the local ballet teacher squeezing the organic tomatoes. We look at her perky breasts and tight behind and we feel like an overripe watermelon. We feel huge and sloppy. We feel powerless. We wonder who would ever want to be with us. Such feelings can lead us to become a victim of seduction. When we focus so much so on superficial appearances, our self-esteem can become so low that if a man takes notice of us, we are pleasantly surprised and become affirmation-seeking missiles. We begin to hunger for a man's approval so much that his flattery and attention can manipulate us.

Not only can we attract unhealthy relationships with men when we feel intimidated by or superior to other women, we also miss out on something we all desperately need: intimacy with our sisters. Whether we are single or married, our sisters often keep us connected to God's love in a way that a boyfriend or husband can't or won't. If we could stop competing and start connecting with other women, this battle for sexual and emotional integrity wouldn't be nearly as overwhelming. Remaining connected to healthy, loving friendships can keep us out of bed with the next guy we meet and help us satisfy our longing for emotional fulfillment.

Every Woman's Battle, page 32

I f I don't cook for my husband, he can go to McDonald's. If I don't clean, he can hire a housekeeper. But if I don't respond to him physically, where can he go? Likewise, if your husband doesn't meet your emotional needs, you certainly can't go to another man. You are not supposed to be filled up with another man's compliments and attention. If we truly follow God's principles, die to ourselves, and serve each other, marriage could be a beautiful blessing!

Some women have tried everything, including catering to their husband's physical needs, in an effort to wake them up emotionally. If this is you, and the above questions have only frustrated you rather than inspired you to try a new approach, then perhaps you both need to look into an emotional mirror with the help of a Christian counselor. If so, I encourage you to pursue healing as a couple.

Every Woman's Battle, pages 150-51

Today I will not dismiss my husband's physical needs. He needs me to meet his needs as much as I need him to meet mine.

Attention is based on what we see, whereas attraction is based on what we hear. Maybe you've had the experience of noticing an incredibly handsome man, only to hear him open his mouth and yell at his kids, brag about his success, or complain about someone or something. Did you find yourself attracted? No. Regardless of how gorgeous he may be, you probably found yourself repulsed. He got your attention, but you felt no attraction. On the other hand, a woman can meet a very ordinary man (physically speaking) and perhaps pay little attention to him, yet she may find him very appealing upon talking with him. This is because women are stimulated more by what we hear than by what we see.

Both attention and attraction are not limited to men but can include a wide variety of things: the kind of clothes we like, the style of house we prefer, and the types of food we crave. Whether or not we feel attraction for something or someone will determine whether we like or dislike it or them.

Every Woman's Battle, page 90

Don't ask: Are my clothes too revealing?
Do ask: Am I dressing for attention?

Don't ask: How can I get what I want?
Do ask: What is my motive for wanting this?

Don't ask: Can I get away with this?
Do ask: Would this be better left unsaid?

Don't ask: Will this hurt anyone?
Do ask: Will this benefit others?

Every Woman's Battle, page 28

The battle for emotional and sexual fulfillment is not an easy one because life is full of disappointments. For some women, every day is an invitation to live in a fantasy world that has no match in reality. So if you are married, you must live each day purposefully focused on building a bond with your husband that grows stronger over time, even through tough seasons. The reality of life is that marriage is not easy, and it requires great effort to craft the institution into the awesome union of love that God intended. Though challenging, the rewards of rich intimacy and deep connection are worth the effort.

If you are single—whether never married, divorced, or widowed—you have a different assignment. You must build a stronger, more intimate bond with God. This bond can produce such fulfillment and connection that you will never feel that you are incomplete as a single person. God's plan for you is as rich and abundant as His plan for married women.

Every Woman's Battle, page 187

Webster's dictionary defines the word *flirt* as "to behave amorously without serious intent." While it may be okay to act amorously (as if desiring romance) toward someone you are interested in developing a mutually beneficial relationship with, flirting is a different matter. Flirting could also be called "teasing," as the person doing the flirting has no serious intent. Regardless of her marital status, should a woman stir up a man (emotionally or physically) when she has no intention of pursuing a relationship with him? Is it loving to tease someone with your attentions and affections if you have no desire to fulfill any hopes you may arouse? Showing a sincere love and respect for others allows no room for flirting or teasing.

Every Woman's Battle, pages 104-5

Lord, make me more aware of when I am flirting and how it affects the other person involved. Help me show that person love and respect without raising his hopes, causing him to form expectations, or stirring up feelings that I have no interest in returning.

I f you've gone too far sexually, whether you did so intentionally or accidentally, you can have a fresh start as well. Don't focus on your past failures. God is merciful and wants to draw you back into a love relationship with Him no matter how far down the wrong path you've traveled. Ask Him to forgive you and to guide you down a better path. Jesus Christ died to give you a clean slate—your free gift for the taking. Simply focus on your future success as you experience the Holy Spirit giving you the strength to live a life of sexual integrity.

Every Young Woman's Battle, page 188

Or don't you know that all of us who were baptized into Christ Jesus were baptized into his death? We were therefore buried with him through baptism into death in order that, just as Christ was raised from the dead through the glory of the Father, we too may live a new life. (ROMANS 6:3-4)

For a Christian woman, sexual and emotional integrity means that her thoughts, words, emotions, and actions all reflect an inner beauty and a sincere love for God, others, and herself. Not that she is never tempted to think, say, feel, or do something inappropriate, but she tries diligently to resist these temptations and stand firm in her convictions. She doesn't use men in an attempt to get her emotional cravings met, or entertain sexual or romantic fantasies about men she is not married to. She doesn't compare her husband to other men, discounting his personal worth and withholding a part of herself from him as punishment for his imperfections. She doesn't dress to seek male attention, but she doesn't limit herself to a wardrobe of ankle-length muumuus, either. She may dress fashionably and look sharp or may even appear sexy (like beauty, sexy is in the eye of the beholder), but her motivation isn't self-seeking or seductive. She presents herself as an attractive woman because she knows she represents God to others.

Every Woman's Battle, page 29

Father God, sometimes I get cross-purposed and remain committed to my own interests. Help me honestly ask for truth to be revealed in my life. Remove those thoughts and actions that are hurtful to me and to others. Instead, please give me the motivation to search for Your face when I am lost. You are responsible for my journey. You know the direction my life should take. Direct me and guide me toward Your purpose. Thank You for loving me and desiring me so deeply that You seek a relationship with me even in my wandering.

Every time you choose to passionately kiss or touch a guy in a sexual way, you are sending a message that he can treat you like his little plaything. Every time you hold on to your boundaries, you teach him that you are a woman of integrity who is worth the wait. If he is too impatient to wait until marriage, then *he's* risky marriage material anyway. If you are too impatient to wait until marriage, you are learning patterns that make you risky marriage material too. You want to be able to trust each other wholeheartedly, and dating is a season in which you earn that trust.

Every Young Woman's Battle, page 188

When God told Eve, "Your desire will be for your husband and he will rule over you," was He saying that women will have a *sexual* desire for their husbands? While most scholars read the first half of this sentence and make that assumption, look at the entire sentence before drawing your conclusion. It says, "Your desire will be for your husband *and* he will *rule* over you."

A woman's *desire* and the issue of *rulership* or *power* are related in a way that unwraps some of the mystery behind a woman's sexual conduct (or misconduct, rather). The desire for power (and the belief that men possess the power women crave) is what causes many women to seduce men, as well as what prompts some to use sex as a bargaining tool in their marriages. It's not as much sex or love that these women are in pursuit of as it is the power behind bringing a man to his knees with her charms.

Every Woman's Battle, page 55

Physically, the heart is at the center of your circulatory system. It pumps oxygenated blood throughout your body. If there is trouble inside your heart, your entire body is in danger of losing its life-giving flow of blood. Spiritually, your heart is the place the Holy Spirit dwells when you invite Him into your life (see Ephesians 3:16-17). You receive salvation not just through head knowledge of God but through belief in your heart that Jesus Christ is Lord (see Romans 10:9-10). Emotionally, your heart leaps for joy when you find delight in something or someone. It also aches when you experience disappointment with or loss of something or someone special.

Every Woman's Battle, page 87

That if you confess with your mouth, "Jesus is Lord," and believe in your heart that God raised him from the dead, you will be saved. For it is with your heart that you believe and are justified, and it is with your mouth that you confess and are saved. (ROMANS 10:9-10)

Have you ever wondered what your Christianity is really made of behind all the Bible studies and potlucks and Easter pageant costumes you've sewn? Your moment of truth is upon you. This is your chance to bring glory to God, your chance to live it all out in spite of the pain.

This is your opportunity to live like a real Christian, to truly sacrifice, to truly rebuild on the foundation of Christian principles, and to truly align your thinking with Christ regarding your marriage.

A man has far more potential for blessing his wife than most women ever dream. As a wife, you can help your husband go there. You must look to your husband to rise up and stand as a trustworthy man.

Every Heart Restored, page 133

We are rehearsing when we think about the conversations we would have with a particular man if we were ever alone with him, when we entertain thoughts of an intimate rendezvous, or wish that a certain man would take special notice of us. When we rehearse these scenarios, we imagine what we'll say and do in these encounters. Then when Satan lays the trap and leads that man our direction, guess what? We are more than likely going to play the part exactly the way we have rehearsed it. When we don't guard our minds in our relationships with men, we weaken our resistance before any encounter takes place.

But we do have some choice in the matter. We don't have to be sitting ducks. We can train our minds to mind.

Even though inappropriate thoughts inevitably pop up into every person's mind, we do not have to entertain them. Such thoughts are not sin, but dwelling on such thoughts is essentially rehearsing for rebellion, and acting on such thoughts is sin.

Every Woman's Battle, pages 74-75

Pride assumes several things:
- I deserve whatever I desire.
- My needs should be met at any cost.
- Life is all about me and my pleasure.
- The rules apply to everyone but me.
- I'm above the consequences.

While we may never say these statements out loud, don't our actions sometimes prove these attitudes to be true?

Every Woman's Battle, pages 137-38

Today I will examine my actions and attitudes to determine how many are borne of pride.

Humility says:
- "My fleshly desires will not dictate my actions."
- "Meeting my needs is secondary to loving others."
- "Life is all about God and His pleasure."
- "I will submit to the rules for righteousness' sake."
- "I win only when I resist sin."

Every Woman's Battle, page 139

Lord, I desire a humble spirit. Not only
will this help in my battle for sexual and
emotional integrity, but it will help me
draw closer to You. The humble knowledge
that I can do nothing without You is the one
weapon I need in this battle. You,
Lord, are my secret weapon.

Have you ever noticed that you feel more lonely and isolated after watching television alone? That's because there was no human contact. Masturbation is similar. There was no real sexual encounter. Sure, the act feels sexual and the resulting climax feels like intimacy, but it actually leaves you feeling more alone and more ashamed than when you woke up that morning.

What an awful, sucking whirlpool of pain. But it gets worse. What you don't realize is that you are rewiring your hardware in a way that will corrupt your future sexual relationship if and when you marry.

It's like a computer virus, only worse. A computer virus can instantly destroy the efficiencies of the machine's software, but the hardware is left largely intact. Sadly, human hardwiring is not so rugged, and heavy wounding can warp the brain's hardware itself.

Every Heart Restored, page 115

Think about the women you respect and admire. Consider female Bible characters, historical figures, or special ladies in your own life and make a list of those who impress you the most.

Why are the women you listed so special? What did each of them contribute to society or to your life? Do you admire them for their physical beauty or their weight or because of the beauty of their deeds and the value of the investments they've made into other people's lives?

What about you? What do you want to be remembered for? Your obsession with your own appearance and weight or your passion to love and serve others? Do you want to spend your life looking into mirrors, distracted by your own reflection and how your looks compare to others, or do you want to invest your life looking beyond yourself and into a world of people who need to experience the love of God through you?

Every Young Woman's Battle, pages 59-60

You are getting into a four-door car by yourself. It's late at night and you are in a rough neighborhood. In order to feel safe, what is the first thing you are going to do when you get in the car? Right. Lock the doors.

How many doors will you lock? If you only locked one or two or even three of the doors, would you be safe? Of course not. All four doors must be locked to keep out an unwelcome intruder.

The same is true with keeping out unwelcome sexual temptations. These temptations can invade our lives and eventually give birth to sin in four ways: the thoughts we choose to entertain, the words we speak or the conversations we engage in, the failure to guard our hearts from unhealthy relationships, and allowing our bodies to be in the wrong place at the wrong time with the wrong person.

Even if we leave only one of these doors unlocked, we are vulnerable. We must guard all four areas (our minds, our mouths, our hearts, and our bodies) if we have any hope of remaining safe and maintaining sexual integrity.

Every Woman's Battle, page 67

The banking industry invests a considerable amount of time training its employees to recognize counterfeit bills. Rather than introducing a variety of counterfeits and teaching employees how to recognize those, they have employees spend a great amount of time handling nothing but genuine currency. The logic is that if you know the real thing by heart, you'll never accept an imitation.

The same principle applies to intimacy in marriage. Once you understand what a priceless gift your sexuality is and how it can bond you and your husband in a way that you'll never experience outside of marriage, you'll be far less likely to settle for anything less than God's plan for sexual and emotional fulfillment.

Every Woman's Battle, page 143

For this reason a man will leave his father
and mother and be united to his wife, and
they will become one flesh. The man and his
wife were both naked, and they felt no shame.
(GENESIS 2:24-25)

Respecting your husband is your highest calling as a wife. No, he hasn't always made it easy, but it is still your calling, and Christ still expects you to do it for Him, even when you can't do it for your husband.

Respecting your husband takes on many forms, but you know that respecting him sexually means trying your best to make sure he's fulfilled, putting your whole self into it each time you're together, and making sure by your actions that he knows that you like sex with him. A wife's respect in the sexual arena is very important to her husband's self-esteem, and he is happier and more contented—and more able to handle a heavy load of stress with a wife, four kids, and his careers—if he knows he has your respect.

Every Heart Restored, pages 72-73

Imagine wanting to give a squirrel a nut. How would you do it? Would you chase the squirrel around the yard, grab him by his scrawny neck, and force the nut into his chubby cheeks? Of course not. You cannot require a squirrel to take a nut from you. However, you can inspire the squirrel by simply placing a nut in your open palm, lying down beneath a tree, and falling asleep. When it's the squirrel's idea to take the nut, he'll do it.

Communicating intimately with your husband is very similar to giving a squirrel a nut. Requiring it is futile, but it can be inspired.

Every Woman's Battle, page 145

No relationship is beyond repair when two people begin serving each other unselfishly. God sees the desires of your heart for intimacy and will honor your faithfulness. Many men get a revelation of their wives' emotional needs even after years of confusion and chaos in their marriage. If your husband needs a revelation such as this, remember these three points:

- Revelation doesn't come through human means but through divine means.
- If your heart has become bitter or resentful of your husband's lack of sensitivity to your emotional needs, pray for God to help you get your heart in the right place to inspire improvement.
- Make every attempt to satisfy his sexual needs.

Every Woman's Battle, page 151

Lord, help us through this. Give my husband an understanding of my emotional needs. Help me get my heart in the right place so that he will want to improve our marriage. Help us serve each other. With Your help we can heal this relationship.

Another unique difference between men and women is that many men are capable of giving their bodies to a partner without feeling the need to give their mind, heart, or soul, whereas women are relatively unable to do this. He can enjoy the act of sex without committing his heart or bonding spiritually with the object of his physical desire. A woman's body, however, goes only to someone who she thinks of night and day and with whom her heart and spirit have already connected. When she gives her mind, heart, and soul, her body is usually right behind. The four are intricately connected.

Every Woman's Battle, pages 13-14

Lord, thank You for the way You made me.
Thank You that my sexuality is an act of my
whole being, not just my physical self. Help
me truly understand the way You have
made me so I may better guard myself
against compromise.

Father, I'm not sure I've even begun to understand what pride really is, but I know enough to realize that my heart is filled with it. There is no doubt that self is planted firmly in the middle of the majority of my motives, my thoughts, and my desires. Set me free from me, Lord! Let my thoughts and actions be about You and about others. Help me recognize pride in my life by thoroughly knowing and understanding Your humility.

*I myself will tend my sheep and have them
lie down, declares the Sovereign LORD.*

EZEKIEL 34:15

Although sheep know the shepherd's voice and will follow him, they have no idea what the heart of the shepherd feels for them. Sheep are unable to share the shepherd's dreams and hopes. They are merely concerned with their daily need for food and water. While it is important for us to follow and trust God as our caretaker and provider just as a sheep follows a shepherd, God longs for us to have far more with Him.

Every Woman's Battle, page 165

For this is what the Sovereign LORD says: I myself will search for my sheep and look after them. As a shepherd looks after his scattered flock when he is with them, so will I look after my sheep. I will rescue them from all the places where they were scattered on a day of clouds and darkness. I will bring them out from the nations and gather them from the countries, and I will bring them into their own land. I will pasture them on the mountains of Israel, in the ravines and in all the settlements in the land. I will tend them in a good pasture, and the mountain heights of Israel will be their grazing land. (EZEKIEL 34:11-14)

Here are some conversation guidelines:

Keep the topics of conversation at the same level as you would if someone else were standing there. Just because no one is in earshot, it doesn't give you an excuse to go to personal or intimate levels of conversation. As much as women like to go deep with their conversations, it isn't always wise. Before you venture into any given topic with a man, check your motivation to make sure you don't have a hidden agenda, such as using him as a sounding board, testing his personal resolve, or looking to get your ego stroked.

If a man tries to engage you in a conversation that seems flirtatious or even borderline (it could easily go in an inappropriate direction), respond minimally and then find a distraction to pull you from the conversation altogether. This will send the message plainly but politely that you are not interested in playing his game.

If a male workman shows up without a partner and you are home alone, phone a friend and ask if she can come over for a few minutes to enjoy a cup of tea—now! If a friend is not available, avoid more conversation than is absolutely necessary while this man is in your home.

Every Woman's Battle, pages 113-14

Perfect beauty comes as a gift from the Lord to all who believe in Him, not from flawless skin, bleached teeth, or size zero jeans. God still bestows beauty on us—spiritual and physical beauty—so that we can bring glory and attention to Him as our Creator, not to ourselves. We are to trust in Him for the things we want (such as attention and affection in healthy relationships), not in our physical beauty.

When we forget that beauty comes from a heart that loves God, we assume that beauty comes from a body that looks a certain way. What if your body doesn't look like the image of beauty that you have in your mind? What effect can that have on your self-image and your relationships?

Every Woman's Battle, pages 54-55

You became very beautiful and rose to be a queen. And your fame spread among the nations on account of your beauty, because the splendor I had given you made your beauty perfect, declares the Sovereign LORD.

But you trusted in your beauty and used your fame to become a prostitute. You lavished your favors on anyone who passed by and your beauty became his. (EZEKIEL 16:13-15)

God wants us to be more concerned with our hearts than with our appearance. The story of the wife of noble character (also known as the Proverbs 31 woman) echoes the same principle but also promises that God will honor such integrity:

> Charm is deceptive, and beauty is fleeting;
>> but a woman who fears the LORD is to be
>>> praised. (PROVERBS 31:30)

Remember, your figure will eventually fall south. Your skin will someday shrivel, no matter how good your moisturizer is. Your body will most assuredly return to dust. But the godly legacy of integrity and modesty that you leave behind to your children, grandchildren, and the women you influence will last far beyond the grave.

Every Woman's Battle, page 120

Today I will be aware that my appearance is only temporary. I will focus on eternal things, presenting myself so as to bring glory and honor to the Lord, not to myself.

For most men, sensitivity does not come naturally. Believe it or not, your husband probably doesn't realize that he is being sexually insensitive at all. Guys just naturally assume that if they are happy and satisfied, then their wives are happy and satisfied. So, while she thinks this selfish behavior should be obvious to him, it really isn't. Their wiring doesn't pick up signals like this very well, and this is critical for you to understand.

If a wife doesn't quietly and rationally explain to her husband that his type of lovemaking is more about making it good for him than about making it good for both of them, he may not get it. While it may seem unromantic to have to do so, you should explain how and what makes it good for you and explain why your desire is much lower now because of his behavior. Don't be afraid to be a mentor in this area. After all, if it isn't you, who's it going to be?

Every Heart Restored, pages 79-80

Historically, waving a white flag in the midst of battle is a symbol of surrender. A white flag symbolizes that the troops are no longer posting their own colors, but a neutral color as a sign of defeat. However, the white flag you will be waving as you surrender your past pain, present pride, and future fear is *not* a symbol of defeat. It is a symbol of victory, for it represents purity. You will be washed clean of all compromise as you allow God to transform your heart and mind into a woman who forgives her debtors, walks in humility, and faces the future with confidence in her Creator and Sustainer.

White is your color, girlfriend! Post it proudly and enjoy the peacefulness and fulfillment of sweet surrender to the Savior.

Every Woman's Battle, pages 141-42

Humble yourselves, therefore, under God's mighty hand, that he may lift you up in due time. Cast all your anxiety on him because he cares for you. (1 PETER 5:6-7)

Society has twisted our minds into thinking that if we are drawn to someone, we must want to have sex with him. But attraction isn't necessarily sexual. Why are we attracted to some people and not to others? The reasons vary from person to person and are many times based on your experiences growing up. Certain people simply "fit your mold," and each person's mold is different. That is why you may have heard a friend rant and rave over her new boyfriend, but you met him and thought, *What on earth does she see in him?* He fits her mold. He doesn't fit yours.

If you meet someone who fits your mold, should you panic, thinking you are going to fall into an emotional affair with him because you find him attractive? Attraction is all part of being human. You must simply exercise caution by continuing to monitor your motives and feelings for this person.

Every Woman's Battle, pages 90-91

Today, if I find someone attractive, I will pay special attention to my motives and feelings for this person, to make sure that my attraction does not progress to affection.

God has given the three stages of *attention, attraction,* and *affection* for both single and married women to enjoy in a wide variety of appropriate relationships, but we must be keenly discerning about this stage. While physical arousal is easy to detect, emotional arousal can be trickier to recognize and even more difficult to control. Emotional arousal occurs when we are stirred romantically by someone, and it usually precedes most sexual activity because the heart determines the direction of the mind and body.

If you are single and hoping to develop a serious relationship with an interested, available man, emotional arousal and attachment is a natural, appropriate part of the courtship process. As you progress toward the altar, you will more than likely become deliriously excited at the thought of becoming this man's bride. There is no sin in being emotionally aroused by the man you hope to commit your life to.

But if you are married, feelings of arousal and attachment toward another man are sure signs that you had better stop before you crash.

Every Woman's Battle, page 93

By letting go of your expectations for your husband to meet your emotional needs and redirecting your focus on meeting his needs instead (whether those needs be for plenty of sleep or for physical pleasure), you are serving him. In this way, his desire will eventually be to serve you as well. He'll recognize your desire to meet his needs, and that desire will be contagious if you do not abort the process by becoming impatient or expecting too much too soon. Just like intimacy, wholehearted service is inspired, not required.

When I speak of serving your husband, I'm not referring to the kind of serving you do in tennis, where you hit the ball to him and now claim, "Hey, the ball's in your court! It's your turn to serve me!" I'm referring to serving your husband's needs out of deep love and committed friendship, with no hidden motive and expecting nothing in return.

Every Woman's Battle, pages 146-47

My command is this: Love each other as I have loved you. Greater love has no one than this, that [she] lay down [her] life for [her] friends.
(JOHN 15:12-13)

What was God's intent? That neither party would have total control of their yes or their no in the marriage bed. For instance, sex under the total control of the husband's yes isn't God's plan. If the husband is consistently forcing his wife to have sex against her will, then something is wrong with the relationship.

At the same time, the wife can't have full control of her no, always waiting until she's in the mood. If the husband is being consistently forced to *not* have sex against his will, then something is just as wrong with the relationship. Neither is normal, and God wants us to know that.

Every Heart Restored, pages 223-24

The well-being of a married man's psyche is tied inextrica-bly to the quality of his sex life. If he feels good about his sex life, that sense of satisfaction spills over into every other part of his experience. And conversely, if his sex life is floundering, then in his mind, other disasters cannot be too far behind.

Every day a man walks into a world that says essentially, "Prove yourself. Prove that as a man you have something worthwhile to offer." In ways both blatant and subtle, a man is evaluated and measured and stacked up against the next guy all day long. The big question in his mind, conscious or not, is whether he is man enough. Does he have what it takes to win the golf tournament, get the promotion, or woo the woman? Successful, adequate sex certainly isn't the only route to affirmation, but it surely is the quickest and most direct one for a man.

You husband may be great at his job, and his peers may see him as a great role model in business, but if he's not too desirable to you in the bedroom, in his mind it's only a matter of time until everyone else discovers that he's not as competent as everyone thought he was.

Every Heart Restored, page 73

Your honesty with your husband about your battle will create an environment where he finally feels safe to discuss his innermost sexual struggles. Make a pact that you won't judge him for how he is prone to visual stimulation and that he won't judge you for how you are prone to emotional stimulation. Your unconditional love can inspire him to guard his eyes, and his unconditional love can inspire you to guard your heart. Consider taking off the mask and allowing him see the good, the bad, and the ugly. And don't cringe when he, too, takes his mask off. Remember, we are all human beings with our own unique struggles. Your marriage can be a place where you and your spouse can sharpen each other with accountability, not stab each other with judgment.

Every Woman's Battle, page 158

Lord, these are hard words. I'm not sure I'm strong or loving enough not to judge my spouse. We'll need Your help, Lord, to keep from judging each other. Give us both the strength to share our struggles with each other and the ability to help each other as we fight our battles. Together we will be strong, and with You we will be even stronger.

Scripture often refers to the church as the *bride* of Christ. If you have received Christ as Savior, you are His betrothed. John obviously understood God's desire to betroth us to Himself in this type of intimate bride-and-groom relationship. He writes:

> Let us rejoice and be glad
> and give him glory!
> For the wedding of the Lamb has come,
> and his bride has made herself ready....

> Then the angel said to me, "Write: 'Blessed are those who are invited to the wedding supper of the Lamb!'" (REVELATION 19:7,9)

What began as an engagement relationship between God and His own in the Garden of Eden will finally be consummated at the wedding supper of the Lamb when Jesus Christ returns to claim His bride (the church). His bridegroom love for us is very real!

Every Woman's Battle, pages 167-68

Some would say that you have no right to change your husband. Baloney! Of course you have that right and, because of your role as helpmate, you also have the *responsibility* before God to insist upon change. If he claims Christ but continues to harbor sin, he pollutes your stream. You are *one flesh,* and because your lives are so intertwined spiritually, you have as much right to expect him to change as you have the right and responsibility to inspect yourself and change. In marriage, your spiritual health depends not only upon your choices but also upon his. You have every right to insist that he handle that responsibility well, in one form or another. You're one.

Every Heart Restored, page 160

Lord, help me go about this the right way. I don't want to be a nagger. I don't want to bring my husband down. I want to lift him up, inspire him to be more like You. Open my eyes to my own condition. Show me where I need to change and better myself, in order to help him better himself.

Father, emotions can be unstable and unpredictable. I sometimes suffer powerful feelings of guilt, confusion, and despair. These dark thoughts cloud my ability to see the brilliant future You have planned for me and can leave me feeling hopeless. Write Your name upon my heart. Help me recognize the difference between truth and feeling. Give me the strength to fight the darkness, to speak truth, and to patiently wait for the emotional storms to break. Guide me toward seeking the help and fellowship I need in these times of overwhelming frustration, and send me Your peace.

Although the gift inside a woman (her heart and soul) is of great worth, the wrapping is what holds men's interest and motivates their actions. Men who value the wrapping more than the gift inside are bad company. As women of great worth, pearls of great price, we have every right to refuse to grace such men with our presence, and we must learn to exercise this right.

Determine not to give away the gift of your presence to anyone who wants it. Remember, you are a pearl of great price, a woman to be treasured. By being careful about the company you keep, you can ensure that your temple of the Holy Spirit is well protected.

Every Woman's Battle, pages 122-23

A wife of noble character who can find?
    She is worth far more than rubies.
        (PROVERBS 31:10)

Here are some personal boundaries to consider:

Save your hugs for girlfriends and immediate family members. Rarely is a hug absolutely necessary with a male friend when a handshake, a pat on the back, or a smile will do. If you decide that a hug is appropriate, give a "brother hug", which is initiated standing beside a person with your arm around his shoulder for a quick side-by-side squeeze or pat on the back. If a man comes at you face to face and initiates a hug from you unexpectedly, simply lean your body forward so that he hugs your neck rather than your body.

When venturing anywhere, whether it is across town, across the campus, or across the hallway, make sure you do not go out of your way to run into guys who always compliment you or make you feel good. Certain gentlemen are extremely fun to be with, and it is easy to be tempted to place ourselves in their paths just to get our emotional basket filled or our ego stroked. But putting ourselves in their paths also means walking down Temptation Trail.

Every Woman's Battle, page 127

Perhaps you've never really considered God as someone who needs a wife, but guess what He calls anyone who believes in Him and belongs to His church: the bride of Christ.

Even though God can do anything without our help, He chooses to do things *through* us. His greatest desire for humans is for them to be His hands to reach out to those in need of His touch, His feet to go wherever He leads, and His mouthpiece to reveal His words and His will to others. He needs a helpmate, a Mrs. Right, to accomplish His goals and pursue His dreams with Him.

Partnering with God brings a far greater reward and sense of fulfillment than any other pursuit you could imagine.

Every Young Woman's Battle, pages 207-8

Let us rejoice and be glad
    and give him glory!
For the wedding of the Lamb has come,
    and his bride has made herself ready.
      (REVELATION 19:7)

You are living in a culture that does not value sexual integrity and purity. Instead, it values instant gratification and pleasure at all costs. Some of you have begun to live by the values of this culture. You have abandoned what you know to be right deep down inside. You have stopped listening to the small voice inside of you that wants to guide you to stay pure and live with self-respect and high self-esteem. Perhaps you no longer resist the sexual advances of men, or perhaps you have become the aggressor. You may be the one going after the men and participating in sexual behavior that dishonors God, your family, and yourself. If you have, God will give you a second chance and put you in the path to healing. If you have not, you can develop a defense for yourself, your reputation, and the life God intends you to live.

Every Young Woman's Battle, page 2

One of the first complete sentences my daughter learned to formulate as a toddler was, "Me do it by mine elf!" I applauded Erin's desire to be self-sufficient, except when her desire to be independent outweighed her ability to manage on her own.

She often refused to hold my hand while walking because she wanted to walk by herself. Occasionally she would momentarily get lost in the shuffle of a crowd or would fall facedown on the sidewalk, crying for Mommy or Daddy to pick her up. While this may sound like irresponsible parenting, we knew that forcing her to hold our hand would teach her nothing. Allowing her to stumble and fall a little would teach her not to be too proud to ask for help when she needed it. Our heavenly Father does the same with us. He never *forces* us to take His hand but allows us to experience the need for His hand so that we will *desire* it. When we tell ourselves, *I can handle this battle on my own, I don't need help, I can manage without accountability,* we set ourselves up for a fall.

Every Woman's Battle, page 136

We don't want to leave you with the impression that God just creates these long lists of rules to make things hard for you, boss you around, or rob you of your fun. Your complete abstinence from all sexual activity before marriage, not just intercourse, is so vitally important to God because your purity and holiness are top priority to Him. Why? Because it is only through purity and holiness that we discover the overcoming, abundant life of freedom from sin and ultimate joy that God desires for us. Remember, He loves us so much more than we could imagine—even more than we love ourselves. He wants you to avoid trying to get around the "no sex until marriage" rule for five reasons:

1. Perfect physical health.
2. Perfect mental health.
3. Perfect emotional health
4. Perfect spiritual health.
5. Perfect relational health.

Every Young Woman's Battle, pages 176-77

P aul tells us in 1 Corinthians 10:13, "No temptation has seized you except what is common to [woman]. And God is faithful; he will not let you be tempted beyond what you can bear. But when you are tempted, he will also provide a way out so that you can stand up under it." Paul didn't say, "If you experience sexual temptation, there must be something wrong with you because no one else struggles with it that much." He said that all temptations are common. Because God creates all human beings (regardless of gender, nationality, or economic background) as sexual human beings, you can bet that sexual and relational temptations are by far the most common temptations on the planet.

Every Woman's Battle, page 46

Lord, thank You that You will never let a temptation cross my path without providing a way out. Thank You for the knowledge that I am not the only one fighting this battle.

Consider implementing this practical tip for cultivating genuine intimacy in your lovemaking:

Be open to discussing ways that your husband can enhance your physical pleasure and inquire about the same for him. Often we know our own bodies and what feels good far better than we know the opposite sex's body, and most men are very open to learning all they can about the fascinating area that is intended exclusively for his pleasure. Also feel free to discuss sexual fantasies with each other, as long as those fantasies involve no one other than the two of you. Remember, a woman is most aroused by what she hears, and sensual words spoken between the two of you while engaging in physical intimacy can cause a woman to melt like butter.

Every Woman's Battle, page 155

You have a job to do, one that will impact your future fulfillment and security. The job? To successfully integrate your sexuality with the rest of your life. We want you to be the same person on Friday night that you are on Sunday when you are at church. We don't want you to live a Christian life in front of some people but then act differently around guys. A segmented life brings confusion, guilt, and often despair.

We don't want that for you. We want you to have a healthy view of sex. We want you to believe that sex as God intended it is so great that it's worth waiting until marriage to experience it. We want you to be comfortable with yourself and with others, deeply connected, and free of guilt and shame. We want you to seek, find, and live the best life possible.

Every Young Woman's Battle, pages 3-4

When you go from person to person and indulge in a new "flavor of the month" whenever you get a little bored in a relationship, you set yourself up to always crave something new. Then when you find a good guy and settle down, your old patterns of relating can come back to tempt you. As soon as the new wears off your marriage, the craving to sample yet another flavor can be overwhelming.

So how can you increase the likelihood that the emotional bond you share with your husband someday will be as strong as possible? By being careful not to emotionally attach to a guy until you have enough evidence to believe that he is a man of character and a good match for you as a potential mate.

Every Young Woman's Battle, page 149

Let me warn you that when you experience sexual fulfill-ment on the deep level of genuine intimacy (not just a physical level, but also a mental, emotional, and spiritual level as well), you may notice some strange occurrences. Because of the deep emotional release that experiencing an orgasm can be for a woman, you may find yourself bursting into tears in his arms afterward. Or you may begin laughing hysterically (not *at* your husband, but *with* your husband). Perhaps you will be motivated to put on some worship music and worship together, just the two of you in your bed-room. You just never know how you are going to be inspired to react when you feel so incredibly fulfilled from the top of your head to the bottom of your toes and all points in be-tween (including your mind, heart, and spirit, of course). You may even find yourself enjoying and initiating sex more often than your husband does!

Every Woman's Battle, page 156

How did our culture sink so quickly into this sexual stew? The answer: we've dumped Scripture and lost our saltiness.

As Christians we have little preservative effect upon our culture anymore. We wouldn't be useless if we feared God more than we feared men. After all, what if Christians stopped watching sensual halftime shows and refused to buy tickets to the latest R-rated releases and stopped purchasing videos that titillate? Things would change pretty quickly around here.

Every Heart Restored, page 96

Let me tell you why you are here. You're here to be salt-seasoning that brings out the God-flavors of this earth. If you lose your saltiness, how will people taste godliness? You've lost your usefulness and will end up in the garbage. (MATTHEW 5:13, MSG)

The romantic intimacy Jesus offers you on a day-to-day, moment-by-moment basis is exactly what many women look for all their lives but never find in earthly relationships. Sex with some guy is not where you'll experience ultimate fulfillment. You will only find that by falling in love with Jesus, the One who made your mind, heart, and body and who knows exactly what you need to satisfy every part of it.

Basking in this love relationship with Jesus is the secret to winning the war against sexual temptations. He stands ready and able to help you guard your mind, heart, and body even in the midst of this sex-saturated world. Surrender your battle to God and ask Him to reveal His lavish love to you.

Every Young Woman's Battle, pages 217-18

*Today I will not try to fight this battle
alone. I will surrender myself to God,
accepting the strength His love provides.*

The headlines of local newspapers point to a sex-saturated culture, as do safe-sex programs in public schools, pro-choice rallies promoting legalized abortion, and gay and lesbian rights activists marching for their cause.

What started over a hundred years ago as a women's movement for equal rights, equal pay, and equal opportunity has evolved into something it was never intended to be. We are living in an age where many women are actually more promiscuous than men. Now women are trying to exert power over others, insisting on their rights to make "choices" while (1) disregarding respect for men's rights to avoid sexual temptations and (2) disregarding God's design for sex to create life and to bring intimacy between a husband and a wife.

Every Woman's Battle, pages 58-59

Our God designed males and females to fit together perfectly, to long for emotional connection with one another, and to be stimulated and aroused by the sights, sounds, and even smells of one another. He loves us so much that He designed every fiber of our being to want to fulfill His commandment to "be fruitful and multiply." He created the act of sexual intimacy as a means to provide men and women with physical, mental, emotional, and spiritual pleasure beyond description.

So if sex is so wonderful, why shouldn't you be allowed to engage in sexual activity as soon as you feel ready? As soon as you experience the longing for intimacy and closeness?

Because God's perfect plan is that you enjoy sexual intercourse exclusively within marriage. As much as God knows the pleasures of sex and the bonding that can take place when a couple engages in it, He also knows the painful consequences of sex outside of marriage—physical, mental, emotional, and spiritual—and He wants to protect you from those. The great sex you and your husband will enjoy someday will be free from painful consequences or guilt— and well worth the wait!

Every Young Woman's Battle, page 21

Father, I love You and need You and want You desperately. At least I have moments of desperately loving and needing and wanting You. Would You increase my desire for intimacy with You, Lord? And please forgive me for doubting that You passionately desire intimacy with me.

*His master replied, "Well done, good
and faithful servant! You have been
faithful with a few things; I will put you
in charge of many things. Come
and share your master's happiness!"*

MATTHEW 25:21

While sheep stay outside, servants at least live in the same household as the master and can talk with him, as long as it is business. The servant enjoys a more intimate relationship. This level of relationship is referred to in the parable of the talents (Matthew 25:14-30) and in the parable of the ten minas (Luke 19:11-27).

However, servants know little of what is happening with the master other than what they are directly involved with. A servant's value is based on how well she can complete the master's will. If she does not comply according to her master's expectations, she will be removed from the household and replaced by another. While it is important for us to serve God wholeheartedly and do His will, God still longs to have an even greater level of intimacy with us than this.

Every Woman's Battle, page 165

Imagine what it is like when two sexually pure people get married. He has guarded his heart and bounced his eyes, and she is the only naked woman he has ever seen. Can you imagine how hot she would be to him? And she has never been held so intimately that she knows the smell of any man's skin but his. She has no one to compare his gentle touch and caress to. Can you imagine how hot he would be to her? They can have guilt-free sex however many times in whatever way they want until they die. Now that is what God wants sex to be. No comparison. No disappointment. No guilt or shame. Only good, clean fun between husband and wife.

Every Young Woman's Battle, pages 21-22

We sometimes do not see the big picture regarding the way God designed marriage. We choose to marry based on similarities and compatibility, but when the honeymoon's over, we sometimes believe we've made a mistake, not thinking for one moment that God *also* brings us together for our differences and even our wounds, since living happily ever after is not the only thing He has in mind for us. We're blinded and trapped by our less-mature, lower-ways view.

But God has much more on His mind, and it may not be until all is said and done that we can understand why God brought the two of us together. So we whine, "God, I didn't sign up for this! You promised a soul mate, but I got this instead. It isn't fair! Why did this have to happen to me?"

But we aren't grasping the big picture. Providing a lifetime soul mate *is* on God's list, but how soon we'll *seem* like soul mates on a day-to-day basis depends upon the softness of our hearts to His sanctification work, both inside and outside the bedroom. That's part of God's higher ways.

Every Heart Restored, pages 141-42

It's not uncommon for a wife to focus on her husband's behavior. She watches every move intently, and more often than not, the husband fails under that pressure. It's far wiser to work on your husband's trustworthiness to God by exposing your husband's well-crafted image to the light. Not only does that take the pressure off of everyone, but it is also the proper target. Your job is to help him see and open his heart and ears to God.

You do this by defending God's boundaries and not your own. Be transparent, persistent, and resolute. Say something like this: "Honey, this is how we're called to act, and we really have no choice. God won't let us live any other way, and I can't live any other way." Don't try to control him, because you can't. Just stand normally and in Christ.

You aren't there to attack the man; you are there to boost the man. It's your ministry to bring him back to God spiritually. Keeping this as your focus may be hard, but it's the right focus. This is ultimately between your husband and the King.

Every Heart Restored, pages 190-91

The only man that a married woman should feel emotionally aroused by or attached to is her husband.

How can you tell the difference between attraction or affection and emotional arousal and attachment toward a man? Here are some questions to ask yourself in order to evaluate whether or not as a married woman you are on dangerous ground:

- Do you think of this man often (several times each day) even though he is not around?
- Do you select your daily attire based on whether you will see this person?
- Do you go out of your way to run into him, hoping he'll notice you?
- Do you find reasons to e-mail him, eagerly anticipating his response?
- Do you wonder if he feels any attraction toward you?
- Do you want to talk or spend time alone with this person, out of earshot or eyesight of anyone else?

If the answer to any of these questions is yes, you need to stop and run in the opposite direction from this relationship until your emotions are more stable.

Every Woman's Battle, page 94

While it is normal and healthy to have fantasies, they need to be restricted to your marriage partner. It's okay to fantasize that he brings you flowers or makes you a candle-light dinner or rubs lotion on your back. It's okay to fantasize about showering together or having wild sex on some tropical deserted island as long as it is with your husband! Sharing these appropriate fantasies with your spouse will add passion and sizzle to your relationship.

However, fantasizing about anyone else is mental and emotional unfaithfulness to your husband. Even if you convince yourself that you would never act on the fantasies that include someone outside of your marriage, remember that God looks at the heart (1 Samuel 16:7) and His heart breaks when yours is divided, even if only in your fantasies.

Every Woman's Battle, page 37

Ask yourself, "Do I consider my husband my friend?" Treating your husband like your best friend means treating him as the grown man that he is rather than as a child.

Men don't want to have sex with their mothers. Your husband didn't marry you so he could have another mother, but so he could have a best friend. If you treat him like the grown man he is, you will foster in him an attitude of mutual respect, appreciation, and sexual desire toward you.

Every Woman's Battle, pages 147-48

Today I will treat my husband like a grown man and my best friend, not a child.

If you claim to be a follower of Christ, you won't disregard His many teachings on sexual immorality, lustful thoughts, immodest dress, and inappropriate talk. You will live what you believe about God, and your beauty will shine from the inside out. Finally, you will have an incredible hope for your future marriage—that it will be everything God intended for it to be, especially the passionate sexual relationship you and your husband will be able to enjoy.

Every Young Woman's Battle, page 30

Therefore everyone who hears these words of mine and puts them into practice is like a wise man who built his house on the rock. The rain came down, the streams rose, and the winds blew and beat against that house; yet it did not fall, because it had its foundation on the rock. But everyone who hears these words of mine and does not put them into practice is like a foolish man who built his house on sand. The rain came down, the streams rose, and the winds blew and beat against that house, and it fell with a great crash. (MATTHEW 7:24-27)

Satan loves to use false guilt, convincing us to cross the line between temptation and sin with thoughts like these:

- You can't deny that you want him! You may as well go after him!
- You've already gone this far, what's one step further?
- He already knows how you really are, so there's no use pretending to be a Goody Two-Shoes!

Satan uses thoughts like this to cause you to feel guilty, but your guilt is false guilt because you have not yet acted on your thoughts. You have been tempted to sin, but you have not yet sinned.

Every Young Woman's Battle, page 37

Here are some personal boundaries to consider:

Many men and women of integrity have decided never to be alone with a member of the opposite sex without a third person within eyesight and earshot. If no provision is ever made to be alone with a man, an affair would prove very difficult to conduct, and it is just as important for Christians to avoid the appearance of evil as it is to avoid evil itself.

Be selective about who you ride in a car alone with. The inside of a car is an extremely intimate place (as many of us discovered when we first began car dating!). The feeling of isolation and seclusion from the rest of the world while in an enclosed car provides the perfect environment for inappropriate thoughts or actions to blossom.

Always keep the door open when in a man's office, and keep your door propped open if a male coworker enters your office.

Every Woman's Battle, page 127

"Y ou are never more like Satan than when you are full of pride." Isn't it true? Pride got Satan expelled from heaven. Pride hinders sinners from asking Jesus to be their Savior and submitting to His Lordship. And pride keeps Christians from repenting of the things that cause them to stumble and fall, such as sexual and emotional compromise.

The consequences of pride can be truly devastating. Eve's pride got her expelled from the Garden of Eden when she was deceived into believing, "I can be as wise as God if I eat this fruit." When Moses was leading God's people through the desert, he assumed that God needed his help when he asked the Israelites, "Must we bring you water out of this rock?" This failure to honor God as the only one capable of such a miracle disqualified Moses from being the leader who would actually usher the people into the Promised Land. David's prideful thought of, "I am the king, and the king gets whatever the king wants," led him to commit adultery with Bathsheba and then murder her husband, Uriah, by sending this loyal commander to the battlefront to ensure that he would die. I'm sure Eve, Moses, and David would testify that sometimes pride can rear it's ugly head and bite you before you even recognize it has invaded your heart.

Every Woman's Battle, pages 136–37

As you talk and share openly with God and with your husband, you will more than likely experience a spiritual closeness over time that may awaken your desire for a more intimate physical closeness. If so, you are moving in the right direction. As you both begin to experience this greater level of spiritual connection (and assuming you remain faithful in keeping your mind focused on intimacy only with your husband rather than with another), you will discover a deeper level of emotional fulfillment in your relationship. For a woman, it is these deeper levels of mental, emotional, and spiritual intimacy that are key to igniting a passion for physical intimacy with her husband.

Every Woman's Battle, page 153

Today I will initiate a conversation with my husband in which I will share a deep part of me I have never let him see before.

When Jesus taught that thinking upon sexual things is just as sinful as doing them (Matthew 5:27-28), He was referring to entertaining sexual thoughts over and over or intentionally fantasizing about someone in sexual ways. There are thoughts that pop into our minds simply because we are human, but we don't have to entertain them or focus on them. We can distract ourselves and resist these thoughts, just as we can resist any temptation. Just as guys can learn to bounce their eyes away from things they should not see, you can learn to bounce your thoughts away from things you should not dwell on. Remember that temptation, in and of itself, is not sin. There's nothing to feel guilty about when you are tempted.

Every Young Woman's Battle, pages 37-38

As you are getting dressed each morning, try evaluating what you intend to wear. Ask yourself: Would wearing this outfit be a loving expression, not causing my brothers to stumble and fall? In a day and age when showing more skin is in, when underwear has become outerwear, and Victoria's Secret lingerie is no longer worn secretly, perhaps it's time to rethink your wardrobe.

While Scripture isn't specific about how we are to dress, it does have some specific things to say about the clothing we should wear. God tells us to clothe ourselves with Jesus, humility, compassion, kindness, gentleness, patience, and love. Clothed in righteousness, modesty, and dignity, you'll be dressing to impress men who are truly worth impressing!

Every Young Woman's Battle, pages 93-94, 96

She is clothed with strength and dignity;
    she can laugh at the days to come.
        (PROVERBS 31:25)

*My God, You know my fears. Help me pray
the truth of Philippians 4—that my peti-
tions and praises shape my worries into
prayers, letting You know all my concerns.
I trust that I will sense Your wholeness, that
all will work together for good. I believe in
the goodness that occurs when Christ dis-
places the worry in the center of my life.*

N o one likes being with a sourpuss, a whiner, or a complainer. By nature, we are drawn to happy people who lift others up. Don't make the mistake of thinking, *Well, if I could just find Mr. Right, I would be a happy person!*

Psychologists studied fifteen years' worth of data on twenty-four thousand people and found, "Being married boosts happiness only one-tenth of a point on an eleven-point scale.... Most people are no more satisfied with life after marriage than they were before.... Although happiness rises after exchanging vows, most people return to their pre-marriage level within two years."[1] Marriage is not the answer to anyone's misery.

Every Young Woman's Battle, page 203

> *Today I will not utter, think, or even
> consider thinking the phrase: If I could
> just find Mr. Right, I would be happy.*

1. Carol Potera, "Get Real About Getting Married," *Shape,* September 2003, 36.

Perhaps you feel that you can relate to God as our Father, Savior, or Lord but are struggling with the idea of relating to God as intimately as you would a husband. While some may even say that it is irreverent to relate to God in such an intimate way, God has always longed for this kind of relationship with His chosen people. He said through the prophet Hosea, "I will betroth you to me forever; I will betroth you in righteousness and justice, in love and compassion. I will betroth you in faithfulness and you will acknowledge the LORD" (2:19-20).

So how do we cultivate a bridal love for Jesus and enjoy this intimate relationship that He longs to have with us? By falling in love with Him and attempting to pursue Him as passionately as He has been pursuing us all along.

Every Woman's Battle, pages 167-68

The hunger for sexual connection can be both pleasurable and functional, but it can also be dangerous if you don't respect it and you fuel it unnecessarily. When used properly within the boundaries God established for sex—only within marriage—a woman's sexual desires draw her toward her husband for a deeper level of emotional connection and physical pleasure than she can find in any other earthly relationship.

As with fire, failing to understand or respect the destructive potential of desire can cause great pain rather than pleasure.

Every Young Woman's Battle, page 43

Lord, help me refrain from fueling my
sexual desire before the appropriate time
in my life. I know that the more I feed it,
the stronger it will become and the harder
it will be to resist.

While meeting guys over the Internet may seem like safe excitement, don't be fooled. Cyber relationships can be as far from real life as the fairy tales you read as a child. It may sound wonderful to be Cinderella or Snow White and fall in love with a handsome prince, marry, and live "happily ever after," but that's not how relationships work in real life, and for good reason.

How much did Cinderella and Snow White know about their princes when they agreed to marry them—besides the fact that they were handsome and charming? Zero. Zilch. Zip. Nada. While you may have thought this sounded wonderful as a little girl, we hope you are wise enough and mature enough to see that such tales are based in fantasy, and many fantasies, if actually lived out, have the makings of a tragedy rather than a grand love story.

Every Young Woman's Battle, page 62

We are living in an age when many women are using guys for their own self-satisfaction and are more predatory than their male counterparts. Many are desperate for affirmation that they are desirable and often control others in their pursuit of that affirmation. While it's appropriate and healthy for any female not to want to be overpowered by a male, it's not appropriate to strive for the reverse—*girls overpowering guys.*

Every Young Woman's Battle, page 81

Lord, convict my spirit if this describes me,
if I have used my charms to overpower and
control men. My desire to be desired should
find its ultimate fulfillment in You, not
in men.

Inside every Christian two opposing forces fight each other. The Bible refers to these two forces as our flesh and our spirit. While Christians take delight in God's law, we also continue to battle the "law of sin," which causes us to crave ungodly things.

Every Young Woman's Battle, page 115

So I find this law at work: When I want to do good, evil is right there with me. For in my inner being I delight in God's law; but I see another law at work in the members of my body, waging war against the law of my mind and making me a prisoner of the law of sin at work within my members. What a wretched man I am! Who will rescue me from this body of death? Thanks be to God— through Jesus Christ our Lord! (ROMANS 7:21-25)

Since the early days of creation, women have had a love/hate relationship with men, wanting a man's love but resisting the idea that any man should have authority over a woman. In fact, many have fought like crazy for more power for women, sometimes for the right reasons (such as abuse, prejudice, or discrimination) and sometimes for the wrong reasons (such as insecurity, fear, greed, pride, or self-ishness). The desire for power—and the belief that power over a man can meet our need for security or love or signif-icance—sometimes drives women to use sex as a bargaining tool in relationships.

Every Young Woman's Battle, page 85

Today I will examine my actions and intentions to determine if I am pursuing a desire for power by using my sexuality to control men.

I f we tell ourselves that we can't resist sexual or emotional temptation, we will likely fall into temptation. But if we tell ourselves that we will not give in to sexual and emotional temptation, then we will be far more likely to back up our words with corresponding actions. That is how you become a woman of integrity—a person whose lip lines up with her life and vice versa.

We must guard our mouths as further protection against sexual compromise. Here are some kinds of communication to guard against:

- flirting and complimenting
- complaining and confessing
- inappropriate counseling and praying

Every Woman's Battle, page 104

arital secrets serve no purpose but to alienate you from the only one who can provide the level of intimacy you truly desire. If you keep secrets from each other, you may build a wall between you and ultimate sexual and emotional fulfillment.

However, through humble confession and eventual restoration of trust, you can turn those walls into bridges that will bring the two of you closer together than ever before. You can rebuild on a firmer foundation by opening up to your husband, confessing your sin, seeking healing counsel, and recruiting his help to overcome future temptations. After all, when you believe your husband loves you for who he thinks you are (yet you see yourself as a different person because you know things he doesn't), that's not intimate nor is it fulfilling.

Every Woman's Battle, pages 157-58

One hundred years ago Christians were upset over the private burlesque shows that traveled from town to town. Today young Christian women stroll down the street with pierced belly buttons glaring below skin-tight cropped tops, completely unaware of the effect they are having on men (or maybe they are aware). In 1939, *Gone with the Wind* brought gasps as Clark Gable's famous shocking line, "I don't give a damn!" made headline news. Today, moviemakers intentionally add vulgarity and sexual scenes to their movie just to attract more viewers with a PG-13 or R rating. Pornographic magazines once had to be sought out, found only on the highest book racks in plain, brown wrappers and sold only to mature patrons. Today if you are old enough to know how to surf the Net, you can usher unlimited pornographic material into your own home via the click of a mouse.

However, the epidemic of sexual immorality began long before pornography or the burlesque shows of the early 1900s. Since the very beginning of time, Satan has used sex to create a cultural climate that lures us away from the holiness God calls us to.

Every Woman's Battle, page 52

The next time you are tempted to flirt "just for fun," remember that if you are looking for a safe relationship to pour your attentions and affections into, you don't have to look any further than Jesus Christ. He can delight your heart and soul and satisfy every fiber of your being much more so than any man on the planet.

Make time to get to know Him intimately. Not only will He reveal Himself to you, He'll also help you get to know yourself better and show you the secrets to satisfying the innermost desires for genuine love and intimacy. He knows your needs better than you know them yourself, and He wants to satisfy you fully and completely.

Every Young Woman's Battle, pages 102-3

To enter the process of forgiveness, you must take these steps:

- Acknowledge your anger and hurt. It is very real, and God knows it is there.
- Realize that holding on to this pain only holds you back.
- Consciously let go of any need for revenge.
- Consider the source of your pain: put yourself in their shoes.
- Pray earnestly for those who hurt you, asking God to heal the wounds that cause them to wound others.
- Pray that your wounds do not cause you to do the same to others.

Every Woman's Battle, page 135

You can bounce inappropriate thoughts right out of your brain by practicing appropriate responses to them. For instance, if you suddenly imagine yourself getting sexual with your date, bounce that thought by imagining how you will respond if he asks you to do something sexual. Practice in your mind how you will politely refuse to go there. Instead of envisioning how you can manipulate a man into being alone with you, imagine how much fun you can have together in a public setting. In your mind's eye, see yourself nipping any unhealthy obsession in the bud. Bounce unhealthy thoughts out of your mind and usher in healthy ones.

Every Young Woman's Battle, pages 110-11

Lord, teach me to bounce my thoughts
so that instead of entertaining them and
rehearsing for compromising situations,
I can rehearse acting with integrity.

A s Christians we can never allow our ministries to be left up to the vagaries of our emotions.

Nowhere is that more true than in marriage. Spouses should never wait until the situation is perfect or until their feelings are just right before moving ahead and doing the right thing in relational issues, especially regarding sex. The right feelings will generally follow the right actions soon enough. Besides, if we plan to love our husbands as ourselves, we must make room for their needs and their intimacy. Attaining normal, sexual oneness calls for personal sacrifices—sacrifices that you may have to make.

Compatibility is not necessary for oneness—sacrifice is—and that's something every man—and wife—has to learn.

Every Heart Restored, pages 211, 221

Lord God, I don't have to tell You how good I am at acting as if I've forgiven when I haven't really forgiven the way You do— utterly and completely. I truly want to be free of every shred of unforgiveness in my heart and free of its consequences. Help me let go of the pain of the past. Help me forgive those who have neglected me or rejected me or abused me. Help me forgive the way I want and need to be forgiven—utterly and completely—so that I can move on to the place You intended me to be at this point in my life.

*I no longer call you servants, because
a servant does not know his master's
[personal] business. Instead, I have called
you friends, for everything that I learned
from my Father I have made known to you.*

JOHN 15:15

A friend's value lies not so much in what she does, but in who she is as a personal confidant. God wants to be our friend, and He wants us as His friend. We can experience this friendship level of intimacy, as James 2:23 tells us, "And the scripture was fulfilled that says, 'Abraham believed God, and it was credited to him as righteousness,' and he was called God's friend." Also, Proverbs 22:11 says, "[She] who loves a pure heart and whose speech is gracious will have the king for [her] friend."

Every Woman's Battle, page 166

Lord, You are more than a shepherd or a master. You are a friend. A friend I can come to when I'm hurt and when I'm happy. A friend who will help me in this battle. A friend who will always be there, no matter what happens in my life.

Everyone longs to feel loved, and there's nothing sinful about this desire. The problem lies in where we look for love. If you are not getting the love you need from appropriate places, such as your family or healthy friendships, you may go searching for it with reckless abandon.

But God has a better way. You don't have to put your heart and body in jeopardy just because you want to be loved. You can seek loving, healthy relationships and guard your heart from compromise at the same time.

Every Young Woman's Battle, pages 135-36

Here are some ways to master the media:

1. Think about all the types of media you enjoy—list the names of the magazines, books, movies, and television shows you watch as well as your favorite songs and musicians. Also include any Web sites that you frequent.

2. Ask yourself the following questions about each item on your list.

   - Would I feel embarrassed if my Christian friends, my pastor, or my family knew I was indulging in this? Do I feel the need to keep this a secret from them?

   - Does this glamorize ideas, values, or situations that oppose my Christian beliefs?

   - Does this book, show, song, movie or Web site leave me feeling depressed or dissatisfied with myself or hungry for unhealthy relationships?

If you answer yes to any of those questions, it may be a warning that you are on an unwise path.

Every Young Woman's Battle, pages 128-29

The most popular argument in favor of self-gratification is "The Bible does not expressly forbid it." Let's be honest. When women masturbate, they don't think pure thoughts, and the Bible is very clear about that issue (see Philippians 4:8). We don't entertain thoughts that are pure, noble, or praiseworthy when we engage in self-gratification. Women who masturbate have some fantasy about another person, some scenario, some ritual they play out in their minds in order to reach an orgasm.

Every Woman's Battle, page 42

Put to death, therefore, whatever belongs to your earthly nature: sexual immorality, impurity, lust, evil desires and greed, which is idolatry. Because of these, the wrath of God is coming. (COLOSSIANS 3:5-6)

any women ask, "Will I ever get to the point that I don't notice attractive men anymore than I notice anyone else?" While your awareness of the opposite sex will likely lessen with time and maturity, it will never go away completely. Remember, the desire for love, attention, affection, and relational connection is part of the human condition. It doesn't change because you put a wedding band on your finger, because you have kids, or because you grow old and develop wrinkles and gray hair. The day you stop desiring those things is the day you die. On that day you graduate from the battlefield to the banquet table. There you will feast in the company of Jesus where finally your "soul will be satisfied as with the richest of foods" (Psalm 63:5).

Every Young Woman's Battle, page 140

Being attracted to someone doesn't mean you have to do anything about your attraction. If you are attracted to a particular male friend, don't assume you're going to wind up fooling around with him someday and so attempt to sexualize the relationship. You are *not* powerless over your emotions. You are not "destined" to be with him or to have sex with him, as if you could do nothing to stop it. In fact, you can ignore him altogether if you so choose, whether it's because the age difference is too great, or because he doesn't share your interests and values or because something about him makes the relationship forbidden. You can feel an attraction to him *and* continue to guard your heart and body from sexual compromise by not acting on that attraction in inappropriate ways.

Every Young Woman's Battle, page 141

God gave us these early stages of emotional connection—attention and attraction—as gifts to be enjoyed. He gave us eyesight to recognize the beauty of His creation, including the opposite sex. He gave us ears and a mouth and a brain that can process information about other people and help us communicate and connect with others. God wants us to appreciate one another and be drawn to one another in Christian love.

But God also had a higher purpose for placing a hunger for attention and attraction within our hearts. He wants our heads and hearts to turn toward Him. As we take notice of our Lord and invest time getting to know our awesome Creator, He will reveal Himself to us as our magnificent Lover, draw us into a deeper emotional connection with Him, and stir up a longing for His lavish love to fill our hearts to overflowing. Once we experience Jesus in this way, all other people and relationships soon pale in comparison.

Every Young Woman's Battle, pages 142-43

I f you don't care to be crucified emotionally in a dating relationship, leave the saving and changing of others to the Lord. Instead, simply pray for guys who have a lot of growing up and changing to do before they can be considered good marriage material.

Remember, what you date is what you are going to marry. Be sure that the men you date do not need a character overhaul, by you or anyone else.

Every Young Woman's Battle, page 37

Lord, open my eyes to the character of the man I am interested in or dating. Show me whether he is the kind of man You want me to marry. Help me refrain from thinking that I can change him. You are the only One who can do that.

hough you want to guard your mind, heart, and body from compromise, you also want to enjoy healthy friendships with guys, and even healthy dating relationships or courtship, because they can help you prepare for a lifetime commitment. But it's very easy to go too far too fast, and for that reason you need to go slowly and carefully. If you learn to determine whether a particular guy is worthy of your affection and commitment and pace yourself emotionally, you won't form deep emotional bonds too quickly or inappropriately. You'll never be caught wondering, *How could I have let this happen?*

Every Young Woman's Battle, page 144

Lord, help me find the balance between guarding my emotions and enjoying healthy relationships. Help me know when to reach out and when to pull back. When to let people in and when to hold them at arms' length.

While emotional attachment is natural and appropriate, it's unwise to emotionally attach to men over and over, assuming that each guy you go out with must be The One. To understand why, imagine this: Two paper hearts, one red and one black. Apply glue to each and press them together, allowing plenty of time for the glue to dry. Once the two hearts are bonded, pull them apart. What happens? Black fibers remain stuck to the red heart and red fibers still cling to the black.

The object lesson is this: When you get attached to someone, you will always keep a part of that person with you, tucking those memories into your trunk of emotional baggage and eventually dragging them into your marriage where you may be tempted to compare your husband to one or all of your previous boyfriends. Also keep in mind that some parts of your heart, once given away, can never be given to someone else, such as "first love," "first kiss," and "first sexual experience."

Every Young Woman's Battle, page 148

You must continue to judge a man's character to determine if he is truly the man you want to be with the rest of your life, not just on Friday or Saturday nights. Even though you think you know him well because of the time you have spent checking him out, things can still surface later on in the relationship that are cause for concern. Don't make the mistake, as many women do when their boyfriends begin to show signs of serious character flaws, of assuming, *Oh, but I have so much invested in this relationship that I can't break it off now.* Even after you've become his girlfriend, if you begin to learn things about him that would keep him from being the kind of husband you deserve someday, bail out now, before you walk down the aisle and get married.

The amount of emotional energy a new relationship would require is minimal compared to the tons of emotional energy many women have to spend remaining faithful to a man they wish they'd never married.

Every Young Woman's Battle, page 150

Maybe you've thought, *Oh, I've been hearing all my life that the answer to all my problems is Jesus, Jesus, Jesus! I know Jesus, but I've never felt complete satisfaction with Him.*

Honestly answer the following questions to test whether you've wholeheartedly pursued a satisfying relationship with God:

- Have you *really* invested much time getting to know God personally and intimately?
- Do you read the Bible searching for clues as to God's character and plan for your life?
- Have you given God as many chances as you have given other men? Fantasy? Internet chat rooms?
- Have you ever made the choice to pray or to dance to worship music or to go for a walk with God instead of picking up the phone to call a guy when you're lonely?
- Do you believe that God can satisfy every single need you have?
- Are you willing to test this belief by letting go of all the things, people, and thoughts that you use to medicate your pain, fear, or loneliness, and becoming totally dependent upon God?

Every Woman's Battle, pages 99-100

onsider implementing this practical tip for cultivating genuine intimacy in your lovemaking:

Don't cave in to the idea that it's okay to entertain any inappropriate thought so you can reach orgasm more quickly. Just because it takes most women approximately five to ten times longer to orgasm as it does men, that doesn't mean we should just throw caution to the wind and get it over with for the sake of time. There's something more valuable at stake here than time, and that is ultimate sexual fulfillment as God intended it. Your husband won't be offended by how long it takes you to orgasm if he knows you are focusing strictly on him and the pleasure he is providing you. You can retrain your brain to avoid inappropriate places and concentrate on keeping the home fires burning.

Every Woman's Battle, page 155

Viewing pornographic images merely creates a battle in your brain, one that you'll have to fight all your life. After you marry, you'll more than likely have to disconnect from the mental pictures you've stored in your memory to connect fully with your husband. You don't want to have your sexual desires awakened prior to marriage, right? You don't want your future sexual focus distracted away from your husband by the memory of couples in pornographic scenes, right? Then rather than allowing pornography to control you, control your desire to feed your flesh with such images.

Every Young Woman's Battle, page 121

I will set before my eyes no vile thing.
(PSALM 101:3)

*Lord, hear my prayer. Come to me in my
time of trouble. Don't hide Your face from
me. Teach me what it means to abide in
Your presence, moment by moment. I hit
the bottom, and only You, O God, dwelt
with me there. I pray for deliverance, I pray
for mercy, and I pray for Your grace to be
realized in my life. You have rescued me
from death, and I shall never be able to
express my gratitude. I will continue to call
on You in my times of distress because I
know only You offer wholeness and life.*

Perhaps you've wondered, *What's the big deal about sex outside of marriage? Lots of people do it! Why is this so important to God?*

It's important because He created our bodies, and He designed them to unite with one person—our spouse, in a pure, sexual relationship. He knows that by design, our bodies are physically incapable of fighting off certain germs, bacteria, and diseases transmitted through sexual activity, diseases that will harm us and our ability to fulfill His commandment to "be fruitful and increase in number," which means have sex and make babies! He forbids certain sexual activities, because He wants to help us maintain sexual health and relational happiness.

The bottom line is that God wants the very best for us, and He lovingly communicates to us through Scripture that sex outside of a marriage relationship is not His plan and can be very dangerous.

Every Young Woman's Battle, page 163

To be a helpmate means that you will never allow your husband to drift to his lowest level. Instead, you'll help him be great.

Now, it's not always easy to help a man. Their egos can be maddening, and since you'll rarely seem like a submissive wife while showing your husband his blind spots, he'll likely object to your attitude on some trumped-up biblical grounds. But you are not being godless—you are simply playing your other God-given role in his life.

It's normal. Being iron sharpening iron is part of Christian friendship and fellowship, as Ephesians 4:25 suggests. Like it or not, sometimes you're required to encourage (and perhaps even force) your husband to consider a higher train of thought and behavior in your marriage, and when you do this, it's okay. You are doing your job.

Every Heart Restored, pages 154-55

A servant's relationship with his master is based on business and performance, while love and mutual concern is the basis for a friend's relationship with another friend. Jesus spoke very clearly to His disciples about this deeper level of intimacy that He shared with them when He said, "I no longer call you servants, because a servant does not know his master's [personal] business. Instead, I have called you friends, for everything that I learned from my Father I have made known to you" (John 15:15). Jesus is saying, "I value you, not just because of how you serve me, but because you share my heart."

Every Woman's Battle, pages 165-66

Lord, thank You for being willing to share Your heart with me! It is comforting to know that I am more than a servant to You and that You are more than a master to me. You are a friend.

I s it right to ask women not to worry about their husbands' roving eyes and hearts? Of course not! We have every right to expect normal Christian behavior from our husbands, and when we don't get it, it's normal for us to feel hurt and disappointment. If your husband is not leading a disciplined life, he is robbing you, so you naturally feel crushed. Your trust has been shattered, and being a Christian doesn't deaden the sound and pain of your shattering hopes and dreams.

When your trust is in shambles, there is only one person you can rely on—Jesus Christ. He understands pain all too well, and He's well acquainted with grief. He's here to comfort you and to build an intimate relationship with you, the only one that lasts for eternity.

Every Heart Restored, pages 20, 25

As you use caution and strive to refrain from inappropriate emotional connections, you will regain the self-control, dignity, and self-respect you may have lost if you have compromised your sexual integrity. You can also expect a renewed sense of connection and intimacy with your husband and purity in your friendships or work relationships with other men. But best of all, when God looks on your pure heart and sees you are guarding it against unhealthy relationships, He will reward you with an even greater revelation of Himself.

Every Woman's Battle, page 98

I the LORD search the heart
    and examine the mind,
to reward a [woman] according to [her] conduct,
    according to what [her] deeds deserve.
        (JEREMIAH 17:10)

If at any point you sense a radar alarm going off in your spirit that says, *WARNING! This doesn't feel right!* listen to it. Don't ignore your mind or your heart telling you to slow down. Let your conscience be your guide. God put that radar there. You may have ignored it in the past, but you can learn to listen for it again. If things get a little too close to compromise, let that radar guide you and resist doing things that make you uncomfortable or that you feel may be wrong. If you ignore those warnings, you may become desensitized to them when they are alerting you to real danger. But if you submit to this radar and let it be your guide, it will keep you safe.

Every Young Woman's Battle, page 191

Does God have only one guy for you? Can only one man be your soul mate? Of course not. God does not cruelly hide Mr. Right somewhere on the planet, and then say, "Okay, now you have to find him!" Many men could qualify as your Mr. Right, but you get to choose which one you want to commit to. However, even if you do not choose wisely and marry Mr. Wrong, when you recite your wedding vows he automatically becomes your Mr. Right. It's God's will that you be a committed wife to this man, through good times and bad, regardless of the character flaws that may surface down the road. If you're wise you'll enjoy the exploration season for many years so that you can truly discern the best match for you.

Every Young Woman's Battle, page 197

In this battle for sexual and emotional integrity, it is important you learn to recognize pride and repent of it before you take a fall.

Here are some illustrations of how pride can make us vulnerable to sexual and emotional temptation:

- The rules of right and wrong don't apply to me. I can bend the standards of righteousness because others do it as well.

- I don't need anyone holding me accountable. I'm above temptation or reproach. What I do is nobody else's business.

- If I can't get my emotional needs met by my husband, I'll get them met elsewhere.

Every Woman's Battle, page 137

Be honest with God. Only He knows what is best for you. Invite Him to shine His spotlight of truth into your heart and mind, showing you what you can do to make your mind more resistant even to being tempted in the first place.

Every Woman's Battle, page 78

The LORD is my rock, my fortress and my deliverer;
    my God is my rock, in whom I take refuge,
    my shield and the horn of my salvation.
He is my stronghold, my refuge and my savior—
    from violent men you save me.
I call to the LORD, who is worthy of praise,
    and I am saved from my enemies.
    (2 SAMUEL 22:2-4)

How do I know if it's really love? This question reflects the wrong belief that love is a feeling. Most married couples will tell you that some days they "feel" like they are in love and other days they don't feel like it at all. Feelings are fickle, but love is not a feeling. Love is a commitment. So if you want to know if you really love a particular guy, ask yourself, "Am I really committed to this person?" If not or if your commitment is conditional, then you don't love him. If you are committed to loving that person unconditionally, even on the days that you find it difficult, then yes, it's love.

Rest assured that a guy loves you if his love passes the test of time, and he consistently treats you with dignity, respects your boundaries, protects you, trusts you, and always wants the best for you. But if he doesn't do these things, he doesn't love you unconditionally—and you shouldn't marry him.

Every Young Woman's Battle, pages 199-200

Jesus longs for His own to acknowledge Him, to introduce Him to our friends, to withdraw to be alone with Him, to cling to Him for our identity, to gaze longingly into His eyes, to love Him with all our heart and soul.

What about you? Do you have this kind of love relationship with Christ? Do you experience the inexplicable joy of intimacy with the one who loves you with a passion far deeper, far greater than anything you could find here on earth?

Maybe you are wondering how to get from where you are now to this much deeper, more gratifying level of intimacy with Jesus Christ. Just as a child develops physically until it reaches adulthood, a believer in Christ develops spiritually in stages as we walk down the road to spiritual maturity.

Every Woman's Battle, pages 163-64

n case you have questioned how God feels about homosexual relations, simply read the first chapter of Romans in the New Testament. The apostle Paul makes it very clear that God does not condone sexually intimate relationships between people of the same sex.

However, although God hates the sin of homosexuality, just as He hates all sin, He passionately and unconditionally loves all sinners regardless of the sexual battles they face. Even if you struggle with desires for other women, God is absolutely crazy about you, and His life-transforming power is just as available to you as it is to anyone else who calls on His name for help in resisting sin.

Every Young Woman's Battle, page 220

Because of this, God gave them over to shameful lusts. Even their women exchanged natural relations for unnatural ones. In the same way the men also abandoned natural relations with women and were inflamed with lust for one another. Men committed indecent acts with other men, and received in themselves the due penalty for their perversion. (ROMANS 1:26-27)

et him lead. One of the fastest ways you can get a guy to stop pursuing you is by rushing him into a commitment that he's not ready to make. If he's not ready to commit to marriage, he may simply need more time. Respect the fact that he's not ready and be patient, or move on to explore the possibility that there's a different Mr. Right out there for you. You really don't want any guy making a premature, half-hearted commitment to you. If he says he's not ready, he may be doing you a big favor and saving you a lot of heartache in the long run. If you are patient until he's ready, then when he says, "I do," you'll know that he really does.

Every Young Woman's Battle, page 200

When your flesh wrestles with your spirit, do you know who will eventually win? *Whichever one you feed the most.* If you feast on MTV and romance novels, you can bet that your flesh takes control when you face sexual temptations. However, if you feast on God's Word, prayer, and healthy relationships with godly people, your spirit can consistently overpower your flesh, even in the midst of fierce temptations.

Who do you want to feed the most—your flesh or your spirit?

Every Young Woman's Battle, pages 115-16

Lord, help me to feast on Your Word rather than on things of the world. Help me feed my spirit instead of my flesh. Help me starve out these sins and claim my emotional and sexual integrity.

Women don't usually discuss their sex lives with other women, perhaps because they fear judgment. Unfortunately, these fears are often confirmed as legitimate very early in childhood when you trust a grade-school friend with a secret and she inevitably whispers it to two friends, or worse, tells the boy you have a crush on all about your confession. These experiences taught us that we must guard our deepest, darkest secrets from other women.

Another reason women aren't as open about their sexual struggles is because of the humiliation that comes with giving sex in order to get love. Most women don't brag about the number of sexual partners they've had. That's because for a woman, the relationship is the prize; the sex was simply the price she had to pay to get the prize. If she paid the price, but still didn't get the prize, there is an incredible amount of humiliation that comes with that. What woman wants to announce to the world her humiliation?

Maybe if we knew how common sexual struggles are to women, it would remove some of the stigma behind having these kinds of "issues."

Every Woman's Battle, pages 45-46

*Father, I thank You for women who are safe
and secure enough in You to be transparent
about their struggles for emotional, spiritual,
and sexual integrity. Help them, Lord, as
they seek to help others. Give us all wisdom
and discernment and the truth of Your
Word as we fight the battle together.*

May the words of my mouth
and the meditation of my heart
be pleasing in your sight,
O LORD, my Rock and my Redeemer.

PSALM 19:14

As we realize and accept the truth that we are God's very own children, we can experience tremendous healing from childhood wounds and disappointments. We can allow God to be the Father or the Mother (He possesses qualities of both genders) that we so desperately need or want. We can be freed from the burden of trying to perform or produce for Him when we understand that He loves us not for what we do, but because of who we are as His daughters.

Every Woman's Battle, page 166

But when the time had fully come, God sent his Son, born of a woman, born under law, to redeem those under law, that we might receive the full rights of [daughters]. Because you are [daughters], God sent the Spirit of his Son into our hearts, the Spirit who calls out, "Abba, Father." (GALATIANS 4:4-6)

If you are living with a man who is physically, emotionally, sexually, or spiritually abusive, there are some things you need to do to ensure that he experiences the consequences of his behavior. If you have been told to sit and patiently endure your husband's abuse, you have been told wrong. Sitting and doing nothing only enables your husband to continue to be a man that most likely even he despises. If you are in physical danger, leave. If you are so desperate that you feel you cannot leave, then start looking for alternatives now. Find resources that can help you out of your desperation so that you and your children will not be in danger.

If you are not in physical danger, take some steps to see if the relationship can be changed. This will require courage and perseverance. It will also require the help of others. You simply cannot do this alone.

Every Woman's Battle, page 188

Don't forget there's a Mr. Right who longs for your attention and affection, who stands ready to engage in a more passionate love relationship than you could ever imagine. He's already made enormous sacrifices to demonstrate His unconditional love for you. He comes from the strongest family you could imagine, and His Father set an example of perfect love for Him to follow. He owns everything in both heaven and earth and can provide for you beyond your wildest dreams. He has a great vision for your future together, which includes a never-ending honeymoon together in paradise.

While you are single, won't you take advantage of every possible opportunity to bask in the incomparable love of Jesus Christ?

Every Young Woman's Battle, page 201

Do you want to know what the best practice for marriage is? Living in a family. If you can't live in relative peace with your family and don't have any close friendships, it could be because you are hard to get along with—and a healthy guy will see this as a red flag. Although you and your family may have typical squabbles, are there times when you can enjoy one another's company and do things together without arguing? Can you admit when you are wrong and ask forgiveness? Can you forgive others and choose to love them in spite of their shortcomings? Do people enjoy being friends with you because you know how to give-and-take in a relationship? Practicing these things now is great preparation for becoming Mrs. Right.

Every Young Woman's Battle, page 205

I f you have a steady diet of messages in the media that weaken your defenses in the battle for sexual integrity, we strongly urge you to go on a starvation diet. When you starve your appetite for sin, it loses its power over you. Then your hunger for righteousness and purity begins driving your thoughts, actions, and attitudes.

To starve yourself, simply do these things:

- Decide not to watch daytime or evening soap operas.
- Avoid watching television talk shows that make a mockery out of God's plan for sex.
- Choose not to read steamy romance novels.
- Don't watch MTV.
- Avoid looking at any form of pornography, whether it is in print, on film, or on the Internet.

Every Young Woman's Battle, pages 119-20

More than anything, a husband needs his wife to be his cheerleader. Mr. Right will want you to be his biggest fan. It's inevitable that you will go through some hard times. You may face great losses, such as the loss of a job, the death of loved ones, or even the loss of a child. He may want to change careers, which could create some enormous financial challenges. As a man wades through the decisions and disappointments that life presents, he needs a partner who will be in his corner, a woman who stands by her man.

When you consider whether a man is Mr. Right, ask yourself: "Am I this man's biggest fan? Do I respect him and trust him enough to be his cheerleader?" Make sure you are committed to supporting and encouraging him every step of the way down life's road.

Every Young Woman's Battle, page 206

As you get closer to your Father, you will see things from His perspective, and you'll find that God is asking you a favor, which is to pick up the iron and to apply the dressings to your husband's life. God wants restoration because that's what's best and fair for your family.

Jesus came to Earth to heal the broken, to have mercy on the ones who couldn't stand on their own, the ones who would never deserve it:

> [The Pharisees] asked his disciples, "Why does your teacher eat with tax collectors and 'sinners'?"
>
> On hearing this, Jesus said, "It is not the healthy who need a doctor, but the sick. But go and learn what this means: 'I desire mercy, not sacrifice.' For I have not come to call the righteous, but sinners." (MATTHEW 9:11-13)

Christ always chose mercy when it came to sin, and He's asking you to move closer to Him so that you might choose mercy too.

Every Heart Restored, pages 180-81

Women can be far too nurturing, even when red flags begin to surface. We often think, *But he needs me… I'm just trying to be a friend… How can I possibly* not *help? That wouldn't be very Christlike.*

While it may be okay for a single woman to play the counselor role for a single male friend, if either person is married or spoken for, the plot can thicken into a dangerous recipe for relational entanglement. Or if a single woman senses that there is a hidden agenda (a desire to develop a relationship) behind a man's appeal for counsel, she would be wise not to go there at all if it's not a relationship she would care to foster.

Every Woman's Battle, page 110

Today, should a male friend seek my counsel,
I will be aware of my motivations and his.

How unfortunate are those who have never tasted the sweetness of sexual intimacy as God intended it to be because they have accepted one or two parts as a counterfeit for the whole. Fulfillment never comes to those who insist, "He doesn't meet my emotional needs, so why should I meet his physical needs?" or "She doesn't even try to understand my physical desires, why should I bother trying to understand her emotional desires?"

Every Woman's Battle, page 144

Let my lover come into his garden
    and taste its choice fruits....

His mouth is sweetness itself;
    he is altogether lovely.
This is my lover, this my friend....

    I belong to my lover,
    and his desire is for me.
        (SONG OF SONGS 4:16; 5:16; 7:10)

Consider implementing this practical tip for cultivating genuine intimacy in your lovemaking:

Don't keep score as to how many times each of you gets to orgasm. Your marital relationship is designed by God so that you can complete each other, not compete with each other. If he needs a sexual release and you don't, providing a quick fix (also known as "a quickie") will show that you aren't a scorekeeper but a cooperative team player. Such sensitivity to his needs will cause him to be your biggest fan.

Every Woman's Battle, pages 155-56

Today I will place my husband's sexual needs
above my own.

All relationships are absolutely wonderful in the beginning. Tons of guys can thrill you in the first few weeks or months of a relationship. But only time will tell if his love, respect, and commitment to you are genuine. Do yourself a favor and be patient. Just as a rosebud's beauty would be destroyed if it were forced open prematurely, the true beauty of a relationship can't be forced either. By its very nature, it requires time to blossom into its full, God-given potential.

Every Young Woman's Battle, page 151

Lord, give me patience. I don't want to rush into something I'll regret later. Lead our relationship down the path You have chosen for us. Imagining what this relationship could be under Your guidance is exciting.

As you make every effort to speak respectfully to your husband as your best friend and as the adult man that he is, you may recognize how much more loving you feel toward him when you talk to him. You may also feel as if the scales of communication are tipping out of balance when he doesn't reciprocate verbally to the level of your expectations, which brings us to another way to nurture intimacy: learning each other's love language.

Most men speak fewer words than women speak. But that doesn't mean they don't communicate—they simply communicate in different ways. If we don't understand this, we may fail to pick up on what our husbands are telling us.

As we learn to speak each other's love language, our love tanks are filled and we protect our marriage relationships from outside physical or emotional temptations. When either or both partners fail to recognize and meet the needs of their mate, these temptations can become overwhelming.

Every Woman's Battle, pages 148, 150

Today I will express my love to my husband through his love language, not mine.

As you may know, there can be an overwhelming urge to sweep everything under your heart's rug and to bury the emotion of it all. Like the heart-wrenching scene from *Gone with the Wind,* you naively trust that everything will work out somehow, passionately muttering like Scarlett O'Hara, "I can't think about this today... I'll go crazy if I do. I'll think about it tomorrow."

God already has one naive, blind, broken child on the scene in the form of your husband, and He can't afford to have two. He's asking you to move closer to Him so He might make your sight completely whole. He needs one trustworthy child on hand to work with Him in this, and He wants to make you strong.

Every Heart Restored, page 184

In addition to putting aside some time each day to rest in the arms of God and converse with Jesus, schedule a sabbatical alone with God at least once or twice each year. Based on the word *Sabbath,* a sabbatical is an extended amount of time set apart for the further cultivation of a love relationship with Jesus. Again, God loves it when you honor Him with the gift of time. What better way to honor Him and your desire for His presence than to schedule an extended rendezvous with Him.

Every Woman's Battle, pages 171-72

*Lord, help me make this happen. Help
me find and schedule a time to get away
and just spend some time with You. A day,
a weekend, a week. Whatever I can do.
I know it will be amazing.*

Father, I seek freedom and forgiveness from the sins that bind me. I seek a place of meditation and rest away from the noise and clutter of the world. It is so hard to focus on the things that are meaningful and real. I know I can't force or hurry stillness. Help me allow silence to happen in my life. Show me how to let go of immediate things and wandering thoughts, even a little at a time, so that I may contemplate life with You.

Once a woman experiences the intimacy of being mentally, emotionally, and spiritually naked before her husband and feeling as if she is loved for who she truly is on the inside, her natural response will be to want to give the outside package physically to her admirer. Notice I said *want to,* not *feel that she has to.* Our desire to give our bodies as a trophy to the man who has captivated our hearts and committed his faithfulness to us in marriage sets the stage for genuine sexual fulfillment. Sex performed merely out of obligation or duty will never satisfy you (or him) like presenting your passion-filled mind, body, heart, and soul to your husband on a silver platter, inviting your lover to come into your garden and taste its choice fruits.

Every Woman's Battle, page 153

Awake, north wind,
    and come, south wind!
Blow on my garden,
    that its fragrance may spread abroad.
Let my lover come into his garden
    and taste its choice fruits.
      (Song of Songs 4:16)

If you have felt lost and confused through this battle with sexual sin, you are not alone. A friend of mine has an extremely bright little boy named Carter. At the age of four, he and his mother were in a discussion about why Jesus came to die on a cross for us. Carter, recalling Christ's last words, "Father, forgive them, for they do not know what they are doing" (Luke 23:34), very confidently told his mom that Jesus died because, "We don't know what we are doing down here." I don't think it has ever been said better. *We don't know what we are doing down here.* And when it comes to sex, that could not be more true.

Perhaps restoration and freedom seem impossible to you now. But there is hope. God can restore your heart.

The transition and transformation won't be instant, nor will they be easy. Restoration is going to take some hard work on your part, at a time when you may feel you have worked hard enough and are ready to give up. But your heart can be restored. You will be able to live in freedom.

Every Heart Restored, pages xi-xii

Maybe you've locked eyes with a guy and wondered, *Could this be love at first sight?* No, it's not.

There's no such thing as love at first sight, only *attention* at first sight. Love isn't an exhilarating feeling, it's a serious commitment that you make after getting to know a person through an extended investment of time and energy. While he may have captured your attention, he has yet to capture your heart. That can be done only over time and with your permission.

Attention is based on what you *see*, and while you may lay eyes on what you consider to be a fine male specimen, that's no guarantee you'll actually be attracted to that person. Attention progresses to attraction only as a result of multiple conversations where you get to know the person more fully.

Every Young Woman's Battle, pages 140-41

If we had a dime for every person we were tempted to give our hearts away to, many of us would be filthy rich. However, the wise young woman who takes things slowly, carefully guarding her heart in premarital relationships, will walk down the aisle toward her groom carrying a treasure far greater than riches—a whole heart that is ready to bond with his for a lifetime.

Every Young Woman's Battle, page 151

Lay hold of my words with all your heart; keep my commands and you will live. Get wisdom, get understanding; do not forget my words or swerve from them. Do not forsake wisdom, and she will protect you; love her, and she will watch over you. Wisdom is supreme; therefore get wisdom. Though it cost all you have, get understanding. Esteem her, and she will exalt you; embrace her, and she will honor you. She will set a garland of grace on your head and present you with a crown of splendor. (PROVERBS 4:4-9)

Invest some time getting to know your heavenly Bride-groom personally and intimately. Start by carving a few minutes out of each day to read His word. Hosea, Song of Songs, and the book of John are great places to start getting a glimpse of His immeasurable love. Take a walk alone just to talk with God and be sure to leave plenty of time to listen for what He may want to say to you. Although you won't hear Him with your physical ears, you can certainly experience Him with the eyes and ears of your heart. Look around at nature for clues of His love, such as the wildflowers He planted along the side of the road just for you, the birds that fly across the sky and demonstrate God's incredible creativity, and the ever-changing scenery of the cloud-dotted sky at sunset. When you notice these things, tell Him how much you appreciate Him and long to know Him better.

When you seek a more personal relationship with God, you can't miss Him. Even if you have missed Him before, don't worry. He knows where to find you, and He *will* pursue you. As a matter of fact, he's pursuing you right now.

Every Young Woman's Battle, page 217

In no way do you have ultimate responsibility for what your husband's sexual sin did to you and your marriage. But no one is perfect—especially in difficult circumstances such as those you have been through. The tough reality is that you might have contributed to problems in your marriage (not caused them, but made some contribution to them). For numerous reasons, you might not have been available to him in the ways he thought you should be. You might have withheld sex from him altogether. While that did not help the situation, it did not force him to be unfaithful. That was his choice. Now, both of you have choices ahead of you.

In John 5 we find the story of Jesus at the pool of Bethesda with a man who had been seeking healing there for thirty-eight years. Jesus asked the man a simple question that all of us must answer as well: "Do you want to get well?" (verse 6). Healing is a choice, a choice we hope you make.

Every Heart Restored, page xiv

Allowing your mind to be filled with images of sexually immoral or inappropriate behavior is like filling your mind with garbage. Garbage eventually rots, putrefying the soul and infecting your life and the lives of those you are closest to. One of the primary ways to avoid inappropriate fantasies and sexual misconduct is to resist such images and thoughts by limiting their access to your minds. This will require close monitoring of your reading, viewing, and listening habits, but once you make a habit of censorship, it will become second nature.

Every Woman's Battle, page 75

Lord, I know my mind is full of garbage.
I don't like the idea of all this garbage in
my mind, tarnishing my soul and the lives
of my loved ones. I need Your strength to
censor myself. Help me monitor my activi-
ties. If I pick something up that I shouldn't,
let me know. Convict me.

Y ou will come to understand that your husband's sexual sin has far less to do with you or your relationship than you could possibly imagine. As startling as it may seem, he truly can be in love with you and still be stuck in uncontrolled sexual sin.

You may be thinking, *But he's betrayed me!*

Yes, he has. But that betrayal, as ugly as it is, does not have the same meaning regarding his love for you as it might from the perspective of female sexuality.

Does it make a man's sin any less wrong? Heavens no! The sexual sin must stop because it crushes us. It crushes our prayer lives together as couples. It weakens the spiritual protection our husbands are called to provide for our homes through their spiritual leadership.

But at the same time, if we are to really understand what this sexual sin means for our marriages, it's vital that we understand the roots of such sin in the male psyche and from the perspective of male sexuality. When we know more about those key areas, then we can begin to align our emotions with the truth underlying the sin, helping God to build or restore the relationship He desires—the one we've always dreamed of.

God didn't design our hearts to be completely satisfied in human relationships—only in relationship with Him. Once we get filled up with His love, we will be able to love others with integrity. When our relationships are healthy and appropriate, we can respect other people and protect their hearts as well, rather than just use them to stroke our ego or to get our next emotional fix.

Every Young Woman's Battle, page 156

Lord, fill me with Your love. I'm tired of
looking everywhere for the love I need to feel
whole. It hasn't worked. I still have this hole
in my heart that only You can fill. Fill me
up so I can share Your love with others.

Because of your husband's sexual sin, your marriage was compromised. Sure, you're hurt and very angry. You've lost that warm, cozy image of your marriage, and that naturally wounds you deeply. But in another sense, you haven't lost as much as you think, because your marriage wasn't what it appeared to be. My point? There is a bright silver lining to this dark, billowing cloud. Think about it: you have been living in a false world, and had it not been for this revelation of sin, you might have blindly and tragically gone through your whole life without ever experiencing the richness God intends for your marriage. But God is faithful, and He loves you too much to leave you where you are now. Of course, it's my odds-on guess that this hasn't felt much like love to you, and perhaps you've been as mad at God as you have been at your husband. But that anger is misplaced. Though the revelation hurt, the Lord has proven His undying love for you by exposing your husband's sexual sin, and He stands ready to help you get through this.

Every Heart Restored, page 34

To truly love others the way God wants us to, we must start with the person we see looking back at us in the mirror each morning. Shoot for that perfect balance somewhere between the extremes of hatred and vanity. Adopt an attitude that says, "I love myself because God made me, and I'm growing more beautiful by the day because I'm becoming more like Jesus."

By making friends with the mirror and moving on to more important concerns, you'll reflect a much deeper beauty than any movie star or model, and you will discover a purpose to your life that brings much greater joy than some magic number on the scale.

Every Young Woman's Battle, page 60

Today I will look in the mirror and think only good things about myself. God made me, and in His eyes I am beautiful.

Here are some ways to deal with temptation:

Rather than eyeballing an attractive man (men are not the only ones who have to control their eyes sometimes, are they?), avoid the second look and simply say to yourself, "Thank you, Lord, for Your awesome creation!" Idolatry is turning your attention from the Creator to the creation. When you notice a beautiful creation, just give credit to the Creator and move on.

Meditate on scriptures that you have memorized as a way to keep your focus where it needs to be. A good one to start with is Revelation 3:21: "To [her] who overcomes, I will give the right to sit with me on my throne, just as I overcame and sat down with my Father on his throne."

Every Woman's Battle, page 80

Casual sex is far beyond the realm of what God considers honorable. Notice that God doesn't intervene and say, "Hey, you can't do this!" He gives people the freedom to make their own sexual choices, but those sexual choices also come with consequences. The moral of that story is that if you want healthy consequences, make healthy sexual choices now.

When we reject God's teaching about avoiding sexual immorality, we reject God Himself. Casual sex flies in the face of God, creating a stench in His nostrils.

Every Young Woman's Battle, page 183

It is God's will that you should be sanctified: that you should avoid sexual immorality; that each of you should learn to control his own body in a way that is holy and honorable, not in passionate lust like the heathen, who do not know God; and that in this matter no one should wrong his brother or take advantage of him. The Lord will punish men for all such sins, as we have already told you and warned you. For God did not call us to be impure, but to live a holy life. Therefore, he who rejects this instruction does not reject man but God, who gives you his Holy Spirit. (1 THESSALONIANS 4:3-8)

It will be helpful if you view the discovery of your sin as God's grace in your life. Your sexual impropriety has been like a huge life-sucking tumor silently attacking your marriage. But now that you've found the cancer, there's hope. Now you can pray for healing, begin treatment, and seek a life restored and brimming with health. Best of all, this is your chance to live out the truth that all things work together for the good of those who love Him.

God has set you free to pursue your personal healing. And He aches to see the same thing for your marriage. Here's your chance to live like a real Christian, to truly sacrifice, and to truly align your thinking with Christ.

Every Heart Restored, pages 34-35

Mighty God, I pray for every woman who is losing the battle for emotional, spiritual, and sexual integrity today. For the woman who is on the way to her first rendezvous with a married man…for the young girl who stumbled onto a porn site yesterday and returned to it today…for the new Christian who is so hungry for love that she's going back to her lesbian lifestyle…for the husband and wife who have lost their excitement for each other and the energy to work on their marriage. Let Your Spirit rise up within them, Lord, and let Your love for them and their love for You be more powerful than any other desire they may have.

I will say of the LORD,
"He is my refuge and my fortress,
my God, in whom I trust."

PSALM 91:2

O nce a woman becomes a bride, all other people and priorities pale in comparison to this primary love relationship. Again, this metaphor illustrates a much deeper truth—God desires a level of relationship with us such that we are deeply in love with Him, that we delight to simply be in His presence, that we know Him personally both publicly and privately, and that our focus and priorities become aligned with His desires.

Every Woman's Battle, page 167

Lord, I want to be Your bride. I want to be excited about You, have You be my priority, my purpose. This is what I crave—this intimacy You're offering. Show me how to become Your bride. Show me how to embrace Your love and align myself with You.

For a single woman, sexual integrity equates to trying at all costs to avoid feeding any physical, mental, emotional, or spiritual longings for a man that cannot be fulfilled righteously. She looks to God to satisfy these needs until she has a husband to make these connections with. It doesn't mean she can't be interested in or hopeful of having a husband, but that she tries with all her might to save her body, mind, heart, and spirit for the man she marries.

For a married woman, sexual integrity equates to intimately connecting physically, mentally, emotionally, and spiritually (in all ways, not just some) with her husband and no other man outside of her marriage. Any compromise whatsoever (physical, mental, emotional, or spiritual) affects our sexual integrity as a whole. One infected part will eventually infect all of its corresponding parts or at the very least, rob you of the sexual wholeness and fulfillment that God longs for you to have.

Every Woman's Battle, page 25

You now have a choice. So what will you focus on—the pain or the hope? Probably both at first. There will be days when the pain will overwhelm you, and your anger will drive hope far away. That's okay. God understands, and He won't bop you over the head for your lack of faith. He'd rather hug you and draw you near, if you'll let him. You're His child, remember?

Still, thanking God for the revelation and choosing hope for the future is the first step to your freedom. Sure, your first faltering steps in this direction will be like crossing a stream by jumping from rock to slippery rock, which means it won't be easy. Being thankful in the midst of chaos is always a challenge. Sometimes it'll feel as if you're thanking Him for your pain, which may seem comical and even hypocritical in your eyes. And it may take daily discipline, even moment-by-moment discipline, to maintain a grateful outlook.

But as you discipline your heart to the truth and choose to be thankful for what He has done in opening your eyes, your obedience will kick up a breeze of the Spirit's breath in your life that'll begin to dissipate your pain.

Every Heart Restored, page 35

Remember, you are a child of God, the bride of Christ, and a precious daughter of the King of the universe. Even if someone treats you less than royally or uses you for a purpose other than what God intended, *never forget who you really are.*

You deserve to be treated with dignity and respect. Period.

Draw a line in the sand and refuse to allow your future to be hindered by your past. God has great things in store for you as you seek to discover the true purpose for which you were created—a divine purpose, indeed!

Every Young Woman's Battle, page 77

"For I know the plans I have for you," declares the LORD, "plans to prosper you and not to harm you, plans to give you hope and a future."
(JEREMIAH 29:11)

But why doesn't marriage stop these sin habits? The Bible is clear that what we sow we will reap. Sin comes with inescapable consequences that follow you into marriage.

Victory wasn't granted with your signature on the marriage license. You must fight your battle for purity, and if you don't, you will have to pay the price at the same toll bridge as the rest of us did.

In spite of marriage, don't be surprised when your sexual sins keep spilling over everywhere just like they did when you were single. Marriage alone won't free you. Sooner or later, you'll have to commit to purity if you wants a true relationship with Christ and with the man in your life.

Every Heart Restored, pages 53-54

Webster defines an addict as one who "devotes or surrenders oneself to something habitually or obsessively." You can be addicted to anything if you surrender to it without self-control—alcohol, shopping, drugs, and even romantic relationships. As a matter of fact, romance and sexual activities can be even more addicting than drugs or alcohol.

Many women have journeyed to this depth of desperation, hoping to find something to fill the void in their hearts, only to discover that the pit was far deeper, darker, and lonelier than they could have imagined. But focusing their attentions and affections on their first love, Jesus Christ, is a testimony to God's changing grace. In His lavish love, God's arm of mercy reaches farther than we could ever fall.

Every Young Woman's Battle, pages 155-56

You may have heard some people say that fantasy relationships are much better than real ones, but is this true? Not by a long shot. Perhaps people who pursue virtual relationships have never tasted how good reality can be. When someone knows you inside and out, knows all your little quirks and annoying habits, knows everything about you there is to know, and yet is absolutely crazy about you, it's an awesome thing. Such genuine intimacy enhances your self-esteem, your life, and your happiness.

There's Someone who already knows you that well and loves you that much. He knew you before you were even born. He knew what every day of your entire life would hold. He knew about every mistake you'd ever make, every rebellious thought you'd ever have, and every sin you'd ever commit, yet He loves you so much that He chose to die for you. Because Christ's death on the cross paid the penalty for all of your sin, not only can you never be separated from God, but you also can have access to Him through the Holy Spirit any time of day or night.

Every Young Woman's Battle, pages 68-69

A woman of integrity lives a life that lines up with her Christian beliefs. She lives according to the standard of love rather than law. She does not claim to be a follower of Christ yet disregard His many teachings on sexual immorality, lustful thoughts, immodest dress, and inappropriate talk. A woman of integrity lives what she believes about God, and it shows everywhere from the boardroom to the bedroom.

Every Woman's Battle, page 30

Therefore I do not run like a [woman] running aimlessly; I do not fight like a [woman] beating the air. No, I beat my body [and my mind] and make it my slave so that after I have preached to others, I myself will not be disqualified for the prize. (1 CORINTHIANS 9:26-27)

I magine a big strip of clear packing tape. It's sticky, eager to bond with anything it touches. Once attached to a cardboard box, it won't come off without tearing the box and leaving paper residue on the tape. The piece of tape might still be sticky enough to bond to something else, but the more you attach and remove it from other things, the less sticky it becomes. Eventually, it loses its bonding ability altogether.

Something similar can happen with our hearts when we emotionally attach ourselves over and over to different people. When we emotionally attach ourselves over and over to different people, we can lose our emotional "stickiness." So if you continue to have one boyfriend after another after another simply out of habit, you may compromise your ability to remain committed and faithful to one person for a lifetime.

Every Young Woman's Battle, pages 148-49

We all agree that sexual perversion is rife across the land, but does that mean all men are always looking at you like a piece of meat? Of course not. While every man has the visual hardwiring, not all men choose the path of lust every time they see an attractive woman. Perhaps they were protected from perverted, unhealthy views of sexuality while growing up and never began to objectify women as sex objects. Perhaps they've been delivered by God's grace. Pure men can notice a woman's beauty and still see her as a sister, moving from thinking *She is beautiful!* right back to their previous line of thought.

But even for these men there are things happening inside them that they don't always consciously recognize, which explains why men appreciate beauty so intensely and why they are so curious about the female body.

Every Heart Restored, pages 55-56

A s intent as we are at becoming women of sexual and emotional integrity, the company we keep can undermine our sincere efforts. While we must take responsibility for our own actions, we must ensure that others take responsibility for their actions as well. When responsibility is refused or not taken seriously, the friend quickly becomes a foe.

Every Woman's Battle, page 121

Do not be deceived: God cannot be mocked. A [woman] reaps what [she] sows. The one who sows to please [her] sinful nature, from that nature will reap destruction; the one who sows to please the Spirit, from the Spirit will reap eternal life. (GALATIANS 6:7-8)

or many married couples, sporadic sex is the norm. It shouldn't be that way and, biblically, it can never be shrugged off as no big deal. Infrequent lovemaking serves as a red flag to mark that something's gone wrong.

Remember, for a Christian, *normal* means to be like Christ. While Christ was never married, we know that Jesus was the Word in flesh, so we also know that when we follow the Word of God, we will always be like Christ. And what does the Word say about normal sex?

> The husband should give to his wife her conjugal rights (goodwill, kindness, and what is due her as his wife), and likewise the wife to her husband. For the wife does not have [exclusive] authority and control over her own body, but the husband [has his rights]; likewise also the husband does not have [exclusive] authority and control over his body, but the wife [has her rights]. Do not refuse and deprive and defraud each other [of your due marital rights], except perhaps by mutual consent for a time, so that you may devote yourselves unhindered to prayer. (1 CORINTHIANS 7:3-5, AMP)

Every Heart Restored, page 223

God designed sex to be two minds, two hearts, two spirits, and two bodies united together in a one-flesh union. If you've never experienced this one-flesh union in your marriage, then you are missing out on one of the most earth-shattering and fulfilling moments of your life!

So how can you move from having "just sex" to experiencing a form of lovemaking that satisfies every fiber of your being? By understanding that sex is actually a form of worship to God that a husband and wife enter into together. When two become one flesh physically, mentally, emotionally, and spiritually with each other, it is saying to God, "Your plan for our sexual and emotional fulfillment is a good plan. We choose your plan instead of our own."

Every Woman's Battle, page 152

Lord, Your plan for our sexual and emotional fulfillment is a good plan. My husband and I choose Your plan instead of our own. We long to be a one-flesh union. We long to worship You in this way.

If you guard your body against the weak links of compromising clothes, compromising company, and compromising actions, and integrate boundaries for your thoughts, emotions, and words, you should have a full armor of protection.

Remember that your body is the temple of the Holy Spirit; your heart, God's dwelling place. As a believer, you have the mind of Christ. And your words are instruments of His wisdom and encouragement to others. When you put on the full armor of God and vigilantly guard your body, heart, mind, and mouth without compromise, you are well on your way to reaping the physical, emotional, mental, and spiritual benefits of sexual integrity.

Every Woman's Battle, pages 126, 128

Today I will keep a sharp eye on my weak links and implement boundaries to prevent them from compromising me.

When I lose hope and find myself unable to look in the mirror because of my shame and guilt, Father, I know that I can only call on You. You are the Kingdom, the Power, and the Glory. You can change my perspective. You can give me new eyes to see that I am beloved by You—that You long for me as Your precious child. I am humbled by Your pursuit and at the thought that You see beauty when I struggle to see beyond darkness. The depths of sin shackle and bind me, but You hold the key to freedom and Your love breaks the bonds that burden me.

What if your husband reacted to your need for sharing and hugging in the way you react to him? What if he said, "I'm only in the mood once or twice a month to give you a hug and talk to you in any meaningful way, but I can give you a quickie talk before I fall asleep."

Factoring out the hardwiring differences, these two situations are exactly the same, but because of those gender differences, men aren't nearly as concerned about hugs as they are about sex, and women aren't nearly as concerned about sex as they are about hugs.

When you offer that quickie, you probably honestly think you are doing an enormously nice thing. But let's analyze this a little closer. If a man gets his intimacy from the sex acts themselves, will a halfhearted, "Are you done yet?" experience be fulfilling? While you think you are going the extra mile to help him release some sexual tension, in terms of his *actual* need and desire for intimacy, you're miles away. It is easy for a wife to forget this part because her intimacy is not tied so tightly to sex, and she doesn't experience it that way.

Every Heart Restored, page 67

Don't assume that every strong emotional attachment you feel toward someone of the same sex is a homosexual desire. You may notice an attractive girl walking down the street, you may think your best friend is incredibly beautiful, or you may feel very drawn toward a female teacher, coach, or mentor. If so, it doesn't mean you are lesbian. God wired us to desire intimate relationships with other women, but we don't have to sexualize those desires.

Enjoy close friendships and make wonderful memories together. Feel free to give others a pat on the back or a hug or let them cry on your shoulder when they need to. But avoid talking with or touching one another in a sexual way, and distract yourself with other thoughts if you find that you are fantasizing about such things. Remember to guard not just your body, but your mind and heart as well.

Every Young Woman's Battle, pages 220-21

Even if he loves God, has strong family relationships, is great with money, and has a promising future, if you don't find a man physically attractive to you, don't marry him. That may sound cold, but you will not want to give your body frequently to a man you don't find physically attractive, and it is neither wise nor loving to marry him if you feel this way. In fact, it's downright cruel.

Wouldn't you be devastated if you discovered your husband wasn't physically attracted to you at all? A guy will feel the same way.

Every Young Woman's Battle, page 199

We're not asking you to become powerless and lay down your rights for any guy so he can walk all over you, sexually or otherwise. Everyone needs a sense of personal power. It's healthy and appropriate to use your power to guard yourself against being taken advantage of and mistreated.

But don't use your power to take advantage of others and mistreat them. "Do to others what you would have them do to you" (Matthew 7:12). Respect others and expect them to respect you.

Only God can completely satisfy your need for love and power.

Every Young Woman's Battle, page 87

Lord, help me find my power through You. Your power. My power is only good for hurting myself and others in my search for love. Only Your power can protect me and edify others. Your love and power will put an end to my seeking.

s women, we must concede that in some parts of the sexual makeup of men, they have a tougher battle than we do, because they're saddled with challenges related to their sexuality that we simply don't have. If you can't muster a mustard seed's worth of mercy and compassion in light of your husband's masculinity, it's likely that you are still too bitter and angry to open yourself to the Spirit's prompting in your heart. While that's difficult to face when you're hurting so, you must face it in order to heal.

If you remain bitter, you'll cause as much stress on your marriage as your husband's sexual sin. And you'll have to answer to God for your stagnant, damaged marriage as much as your husband will.

Every Heart Restored, page 126

Do you want to be able to say no to worldly passions? to live a self-controlled, upright, and godly life? to be purified as God's very own? to be eager to do what is good? You can't do these things by yourself. But God can give you what you need when you humble yourself before Him and say, "I surrender my pride. I need help if I am to experience your plan for my sexual and emotional fulfillment, and I'm willing to be held accountable for my actions."

Keep your eyes open for an accountability partner. Perhaps it will be a friend or a sister, a teacher, a counselor, or a mentor. While you may be tempted to look for a mentor who can sympathize with you, you may have more long-term success with someone who isn't struggling herself or who has already overcome such a struggle. Hitching two weak oxen together to plow a field is not nearly as effective as hitching a weak ox with a strong one.

Every Woman's Battle, page 138

When you know people well enough to discern that you are attracted to them, you might feel the urge to express your feelings by showing affection or displaying favor toward them. Signs of affection may be something tangible, such as a small gift or a kind note. You could express affection by doing something beneficial for the person, like helping with a difficult task or offering to run an errand. Affection can be expressed verbally, such as paying someone a sincere compliment or confiding in a trusted friend. We show our affection by taking time to go for a walk or going to a movie with the object of our affection. The most common expressions of affection are a pat on the back, a gentle caress, a hug, or a kiss. (Affection can, of course, progress into more sexually intimate acts.)

As a married woman, you are free to show all the affection you want to the man you are married to, but what about to someone else? When is it appropriate to express affection to another man and when is it not? How do you know the difference? Where do you draw the line?

Every Woman's Battle, pages 91-92

So where should you start in helping your husband stand firm as a trustworthy man of God? Do you hover over his shoulder with a furrowed brow, arms crossed, jaws locked, tapping one foot impatiently, and intermittently glancing at your watch while rolling your eyes and sighing deeply, "You blew it again, pal."

While that may be your first instinct, it wouldn't be your best one. The *actual* starting place is a quiet little spot waiting for you in front of your mirror.

Hey, wait a minute! This thing doesn't start with me!

I am *not* saying that every wife bears some of the blame for her husband's sexual sin. But that doesn't mean she needn't check herself in the mirror once in a while. People are 100 percent responsible for their lives 100 percent of the time. Yet what spouses do or don't do has a direct influence on the situation. A wife can certainly make matters worse, but she can also make matters better if she plays her position well.

Every Heart Restored, page 137

When you spend time with someone, you are giving that person a gift: *your presence.* It's true. The gift of your company is very precious and of value beyond description. Underneath your breasts lies a beating heart where the Holy Spirit makes His home. Behind your face is a brain that possesses the mind of Christ.

Be wary of men who are intrigued by the wrapping but fail to see the value of what is inside the package. They may want to play with the bow…untie the ribbon…peek through the wrapping.

Every Woman's Battle, page 122

Today I will spend time only with people who value my mind, heart, and soul—not just my body.

I t is time for a new cultural revolution—one where we re-claim and exercise our authority over all of creation (including Satan). Once we reclaim this authority and stop submitting ourselves to a culture that is leading us astray, we can discover new levels of sexual integrity, enjoy genuine intimacy in marriage, and experience the satisfaction of our innermost desires through righteous relationships.

Every Woman's Battle, page 61

You adulterous people, don't you know that friendship with the world is hatred toward God? Anyone who chooses to be a friend of the world becomes an enemy of God. Or do you think Scripture says without reason that the Spirit he caused to live in us envies intensely? But he gives us more grace. That is why Scripture says:

God opposes the proud
    but gives grace to the humble. (JAMES 4:4-6)

Until you are married, sexual integrity means protecting yourself from any physical, mental, emotional, or spiritual longings for the opposite sex that cannot be fulfilled according to God's plan. It means looking to God to satisfy these needs until they can be fulfilled in a marriage relationship. It doesn't mean you can't be interested in or hopeful of having a husband someday or that you can't date or have a boyfriend. It simply means that you try your best to guard your heart, mind, and body against any compromise that threatens your sexual integrity.

When you marry, sexual integrity will equate to intimately connecting physically, mentally, emotionally, and spiritually with your husband and no other man outside your marriage. Any compromise whatsoever—physical, mental, emotional, or spiritual—will affect your sexual integrity as a whole. One infected part will eventually infect all of its corresponding parts, or at the very least, rob you of the sexual wholeness and fulfillment that God longs for you to have.

Every Young Woman's Battle, page 27

Each of us has two major roles in marriage. The husband plays the headship role and is the overall leader in the home. He's also been called by God to be the high priest of the home, the spiritual leader responsible for building a normal Christian home.

As his wife, you play the parallel submissive role to your husband's leadership at home, and the parallel helper role to strengthen him to carry out his roles as head and high priest.

Note how God expects the husband and wife to play essentially the same spiritual role for the other spouse. As a high priest, your husband is to *lead* you into Christian greatness. As a helpmate, you are to work alongside the Holy Spirit to *lift* him to Christian greatness.

Every Heart Restored, page 151

Many married women continue in their addiction to masturbation even after they have the freedom of sexual expression with their mate. They can't see what this habit does to their marriage. But think about it. Most husbands find pleasure and satisfaction in bringing their wives to orgasm. If you typically find sexual release through masturbation, you may rob your husband of this pleasure by insisting that he allow you to "help him." If you cannot imagine how this will make your husband feel, imagine how you'd feel if you were making love, and within a short time your husband said, "Thanks, honey, but you are going to have to let me take it from here." Feel rejected? Wonder what is wrong with you and what you are not doing right? He will feel the exact same way if you have to masturbate in order to reach an orgasm.

Every Woman's Battle, page 41

hen your husband needs your help but can't see that he *needs* help, which role are you to play? Should you simply be quiet and pray for his insight to improve, submitting in silence for the sake of peace? Or does the Lord expect you to step out bravely to defend your home and to encourage your husband toward God?

If you only play "submitter" and never play your helper role, the laws of reaping and sowing will be suspended in your husband's life and he'll pay no price for his abnormal behavior.

Sometimes you'll be called upon to stand up to your husband's foolishness to protect your house, and you'll have to trust the Holy Spirit that as you speak His words into your husband's heart, your husband will listen and the fruit of the Spirit will blossom broadly in his life. Your reward will be peace for your house.

Every Heart Restored, pages 151-52, 155

Although we may have fallen once or even several times, genuine intimacy and fulfillment are still within our grasp.

As you learn who you are in Christ, you'll come to understand that you are not a victim of this battle, but a victor! The prize? Peace in your spirit, freedom from disquieting and oppressive thoughts and emotions, harmony in your relationships with God and men, and the sexual fulfillment God longs for you to experience.

As you seek genuine intimacy with the God who loves you and holds the plan for your sexual and emotional fulfillment, I pray that you not only discover the thrill of victory in this battle, but that you also experience indescribable joy in the journey.

Every Woman's Battle, pages 181, 186

May the God of hope fill you with all joy and peace as you trust in him, so that you may overflow with hope by the power of the Holy Spirit. (ROMANS 15:13)

Father, because You are such a pure and holy God, I know You didn't design society to be sex saturated the way it is today.

Its tentacles are groping for us at every turn—through our television sets, through billboards along the highway, through magazines and music, even through people we love and trust to protect us.

I pray, Father, that You would help us become a society that, once again, hates sin. I pray for a reverse sexual revolution, for an army of millions to rise up in Your strength and holiness to defeat the Enemy of our souls, reclaiming sex for its designed purpose—a husband and wife's pleasurable offering of worship to You.

index

Printed in the United States
by Baker & Taylor Publisher Services